Teaching ART

with Books Kids Love

Teaching ART
with Books Kids Love

*Teaching Art Appreciation, Elements of Art, and
Principles of Design with Award-Winning Children's Books*

Darcie Clark Frohardt

fulcrum resources
Golden, Colorado

To Paul, Robert, and Erin—
thanks for your love, patience,
and computer time.

Library of Congress Cataloging-in-Publication Data
Frohardt, Darcie Clark.
    Teaching art with books kids love : teaching art appreciation, elements of art, and principles of design with award-winning children's books / Darcie Clark Frohardt.
        p.   cm.
    Includes bibliographical references and index.
    ISBN 1-55591-406-3 (pbk.)
    1. Art—Study and teaching (Elementary)—United States. 2. Children's literature—Illustrations. 3. Caldecott Medal. I. Title.
N362.F76   1999
372.5'044—dc21   99–33166
                                                                CIP

Printed in the United States of America
0 9 8 7 6

Cover illustration: © 1999 K. Michael Crawford
Cover design: Alyssa Pumphrey
Interior illustrations: Darcie Frohardt

Fulcrum Publishing
16100 Table Mountain Parkway, Suite 300
Golden, Colorado 80403
(800) 992-2908 • (303) 277-1623
www.fulcrum-resources.com

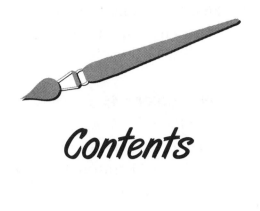

Contents

Part 2: Principles of Design

Part 3: Artistic Styles

Acknowledgments

Thanks to my husband, Paul, for his great expertise in editing and to Barbara McKee for sharing her art knowledge, time, and experience. A very special thanks to the staff and teachers at McMeen Elementary School, Denver Public Schools, whose support and feedback were invaluable during the field testing of many of the art explorations in this book. Thanks also to Marianne Hayes at Barrett Elementary School, Denver Public Schools, who provided such heartwarming encouragement and additional opportunities to field-test my ideas.

Introduction

"One picture is worth a thousand words."
—*Anonymous*

Teaching Art with Books Kids Love combines two activities children love: reading and art. Most of the featured books have won either a Caldecott Medal or Caldecott Honor. The Association for Library Services to Children presents the annual Caldecott awards to the artists who have created the most distinguished picture books for children published in the United States.

The artwork in award-winning children's books is an effective tool for teaching art concepts to children for several reasons:

- The artists who create the illustrations use the same elements of art, principles of design, and artistic styles of fine artists.
- The subject matter of the artwork is appropriate for children.
- The artwork is of high quality.
- The books are easy to find in most public libraries and schools.

How This Book Is Organized

Teaching Art with Books Kids Love is organized around three of the most basic components of elementary-school visual art curriculums:

Elements of Art: Artists use line, shape, texture, value, color, and space as visual tools.

Principles of Design: Artists use principles of harmony, variety and contrast, movement, balance, and dominance to arrange the elements of art.

Artistic Styles: Artists use different styles, such as realism, impressionism, expressionism, surrealism, naive, and cartoon, to create a work of art.

These are not comprehensive lists of formal art elements, principles, and styles. They are simply the ones that many elementary-school visual art curriculums have in common.

In Parts 1 and 2, art elements and design principles are introduced one at a time to help children understand each concept. However, they do not work independently of each other. Like letters in the alphabet or notes on a scale, they must work together to create a composition. A single work of art usually contains many elements and principles that support one another.

Every artist creates work in a very personal style. It is not always easy, or even necessary, to identify a particular artistic style. Part 3 includes categories to help in the recognition and appreciation of major artistic styles used by artists over the years.

Teaching Art with Books Kids Love uses a three-step process to teach art concepts. First, each art concept is defined. Second, examples of fine artworks and children's books are listed. Third, a variety of art explorations are offered to enable students to experience each art concept.

Definitions

The purpose of the definitions is to provide a level of comfort when teaching art concepts. The more you know and understand, the better you can explain the concept in your own words. You will also begin to recognize the visual art concepts in the children's picture books you read aloud. Discussions of the formal art elements, principles of design, and styles with your students will become easier. These concepts are as fundamental to visual art as punctuation and grammar are to our written and spoken language. A variety of information about each art concept is provided:

In a Nutshell: a short, easy-to-read definition
Taking a Closer Look: a more complete definition

Fine Art and
Children's Literature Examples

Famous artworks and children's books that demonstrate the element, principle, or style are listed. Finding the fine art examples suggested can be frustrating and time consuming. Don't spend a lot of time on it. First, look for books containing the artist's work. Then, look for the specific painting. If you find it, great! If you don't find it, don't worry. Trust your judgment and understanding of the element, principle, or style and select artwork that demonstrates the concept you are teaching.

Art Explorations

Each element, principle, and style is explored in a variety of ways. The art explorations section in each chapter provides:

- A book or books that demonstrate the concept and summary
- An explanation of how the artist used the concept in the book's illustrations
- Various activities that allow students to explore the concept

A note on materials and directions: The explorations use simple and inexpensive materials. Most of them can be done with colored markers, glue, scissors, construction paper, drawing paper, permanent black markers, watercolors, colored pencils, and tempera paints. A few suggest oil pastels or soft pastels. Directions have been kept to a minimum. The art explorations are just that—opportunities for students to explore the concept being taught. Allow students to experiment with the concept.

How to Use This Book

From my own experience using the approach outlined in this book, I believe students will benefit most if the following steps are followed in order:

1. Parent or teacher reads the book aloud.
2. Parent or teacher explains, identifies, and leads a discussion on the art concept to be taught.
3. Students and parent or teacher view and discuss fine art examples.
4. Students explore the art concept in a hands-on activity.
5. Students share and display completed artwork (if appropriate).

Each chapter can be presented in two or more sessions. I have had great success with completing the first three steps during one day and the last two steps one to several days later.

As you work with this book, keep in mind that you, as a parent or teacher, are learning as well. Do the activities yourself. Remind yourself and your students that there is not a "right" or "wrong" way to do art. These concepts are guidelines. There are no rules! An individual's use of the concepts in a personally satisfying way is the key to originality.

A Final Note About the Examples

The examples given for the art explorations were created by the author, not by children. Teachers and parents should not expect their students' work to mirror the examples provided. It is not even necessary to share these examples with your students. Creativity and freedom of expression will be encouraged by your flexible expectations. The sole purpose of the examples is to help teachers and parents visualize the explorations and the written directions provided. Good luck and have fun!

Part I

Elements of Art

The elements of art are the visual tools artists use to create a work of art. They include, but are not limited to, line, shape, texture, value, color, and space. The following chapters introduce the art elements one at a time to help students understand each concept. However, these elements do not work independently of each other. Like letters in the alphabet or notes on a scale, they must work together to create a composition. A work of art usually contains many elements of art.

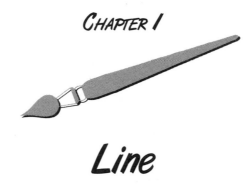

CHAPTER 1

Line

Definitions

In a Nutshell

A line is whatever appears in an artwork in the distance between two points. A line has more length than width and can be straight, curved, or jagged. Lines can be made by a pencil, a marker, a stick, and other items. The outside edges of objects can be lines. Lines are used to show direction and to communicate moods and feelings.

Taking a Closer Look

Lines have many different functions. Vertical, horizontal, and diagonal lines can show direction by leading our eyes through a painting or illustration. The thickness or thinness and the gesture of lines can communicate moods and emotions. Objects in a composition form implied lines, which create organization and show relationships. Following are brief definitions of a variety of lines.

Character lines: lines that show gesture and create moods. They range from very thick to very fine and can be jagged, curved, scribbled, and so on.

Character Lines: angry, frustrated; lazy, calm; confused, disorganized

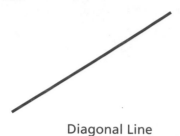

Diagonal line: a type of direction line; any line that is not vertical or horizontal, causing our eyes to move across a composition at an angle. It evokes a feeling of energy, unbalance, or tension. (See *Mirette on the High Wire* by Emily Arnold McCully.)

Diagonal Line

Horizontal line: a type of direction line that slowly guides our eyes across a composition. It can give a feeling of restfulness, balance, or calm. As humans, we sleep horizontally. (See sunset and wheat field in *Grandfather's Journey* by Allen Say.)

Horizontal Line]

Vertical line: a type of directional line that causes our eyes to move up and down a composition. It can create a feeling of growth, rigidity, stability, confinement, or strength. As humans, we stand vertically in an active position.

Vertical Line

Construction lines: lines for drawing an object using basic geometric shapes.

Construction Lines

Gesture lines: quick scribbles intended to show action by flowing around and through an object.

Gesture Lines

Contour Lines

Contour lines: lines that follow the outline of an object.

Cross-Contour Lines

Cross-contour lines: lines that cross though an object and connect to contour lines. They help to make an object appear three-dimensional.

Implied Line

Implied line: a line created by edges of shapes, by boundaries where colors change, or by objects lined up. It can be used as a directional line.

Fine Art Examples

Kenneth Noland (horizontal, vertical, and diagonal lines): *Via Blues, Lineate, Shade,* and *Ado*

Piet Mondrian (horizontal and vertical lines): *Composition with Red, Yellow, and Blue*

Paul Klee (curved, angled, and diagonal lines): *Pastorale* and *Contemplating*

Pablo Picasso (curved and angled lines): *Fawn* and *Starry Night*

Joan Miro (curved and angled lines): *Morning Star*

Edgar Degas, Henri Matisse, Pablo Picasso (contour lines and gesture lines): Pencil studies and preliminary sketches

Children's Literature Examples

Bunting, Eve. *Smoky Night*. Illustrated by David Diaz. San Diego: Harcourt Brace, 1994. (Character lines)

Goble, Paul. *The Girl Who Loved Wild Horses*. New York: Bradbury Press, 1978. (Curved and angled lines)

Ho, Minfong. *Hush!: A Thai Lullaby*. Illustrated by Holly Meade. New York: Orchard Books, 1996. (Contour lines)

Lionni, Leo. *A Color of His Own*. New York: Pantheon Books, 1975. (Contour lines)

McCully, Emily Arnold. *Mirette on the High Wire*. New York: G. P. Putnam's Sons, 1992. (Horizontal and diagonal lines)

Say, Allen. *Grandfather's Journey*. New York: Houghton Mifflin, 1993. (Horizontal, vertical, and diagonal lines)

Steptoe, John. *Mufaro's Beautiful Daughters: An African Tale*. New York: Lothrop, Lee & Shepard Books, 1987. (Crosshatching lines for shading and shadows)

Explorations

Horizontal, Vertical, and Diagonal Lines
Mirette on the High Wire
Written and illustrated by Emily Arnold McCully
(New York: G. P. Putnam's Sons, 1992)

Mirette learns to walk a tightrope from a mysterious guest at her mother's boarding-house. The guest turns out to be the famous tightrope artist Monsieur Bellini, who quit performing because of his fear.

How the Artist Used the Element

As Mirette learns to walk the tightrope and Monsieur Bellini overcomes his fear, the direction of the line (the tightrope) helps tell the story. As Mirette and Bellini struggle, the tightrope is shown as a diagonal line giving the feeling of unbalance and tension. When they become comfortable on the tightrope, the rope is shown as a horizontal line giving the feeling of balance and calm. Also note the diagonal line on the stair as Mirette overhears the guests talking. What might happen if Mirette were discovered?

Art Exploration: Horizontal Tissue Paper Lines

Students use colored tissue paper strips to explore horizontal and vertical lines.

Materials

- 12 x 9–inch heavy drawing paper
- White glue thinned with water (glue-to-water ratio 3:1)
- 1–inch flat paintbrushes
- Tissue paper of various colors, cut into strips of different widths and lengths

Directions

1. Turn the paper either vertically or horizontally.
2. Using the paintbrush, brush a line of glue the full width or length of the paper.
3. Place a strip of tissue paper on the glue and smooth it out with a paintbrush.
4. Repeat, using short and long strips of different colors of paper. Fill the paper with either horizontal or vertical lines. Strips may just touch or may overlap. If the strips extend past the edges of the paper, they can be cut off after the glue dries.

Horizontal Tissue Paper Lines

Variations

1. *Diagonal Tissue Paper Lines:* Place tissue paper strips diagonally. Choose a color scheme such as monochromatic, cool, warm, complementary, or primary. (See color terms and concepts in Chapter 5.)

Diagonal Tissue Paper Lines

2. *Crisscross Tissue Paper Lines:* Place tissue strips in a variety of directions—horizontally, diagonally, and vertically—using strips in a variety of widths and lengths. Choose a color scheme such as monochromatic, cool, warm, complementary, or primary. (See color terms and concepts in Chapter 5.)

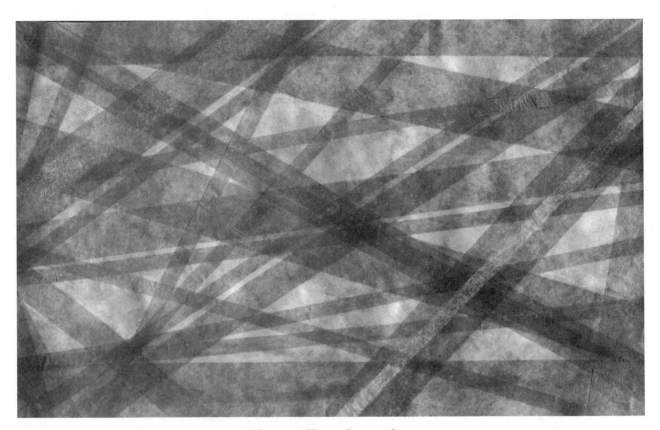

Crisscross Tissue Paper Lines

3. *Stained Glass*: Using a ruler, 5$\frac{1}{2}$ x 8–inch white drawing paper, and a permanent black marker, make a variety of horizontal, vertical, and diagonal lines starting at one edge of the paper and ending at the other edge. Color in the spaces created by the lines. Choose a color scheme such as monochromatic, cool, warm, complementary, or primary. (See color terms and concepts in Chapter 5.)

Stained Glass

Curved and Angled Lines

The Girl Who Loved Wild Horses

Written and illustrated by Paul Goble
(New York: Bradbury Press, 1978)

A young Native American girl chooses to leave her people and live with the wild horses, where she finds true happiness.

How the Artist Used the Element

The artist has used a bold and simple style to create excitement and drama in his illustrations. On the two pages where the violent storm strikes, notice how he has used curved lines to show the rolling motion in the clouds. Also notice the angled lines of the lightning bolts, which show tension and energy. *Optional:* Review vertical lines (cliffs at night and the waterfall) and diagonal lines (tepee poles and blanket designs).

Art Exploration: Curved and Angled Lines Abstract

Students use black permanent markers to explore a variety of curved and angled lines.

Materials

- 18 x 6–inch black construction paper
- 6 x $^3/_4$–inch, 6 x 1–inch, and 6 x $1^1/_2$–inch strips of construction paper in a variety of colors except black
- Glue
- Fine-point, permanent black markers or black crayons

Directions

1. Choose ten to twelve 6-inch strips of construction paper and one 6 x 18–inch black piece of paper.
2. On one of the pieces of colored paper,

Curved and Angled Lines Abstract

draw a long curved or angled line or a pattern of short curved or angled lines from one edge of the paper to the other. Whatever line is chosen, fill the whole strip of paper using the same line or pattern of lines.

3. Repeat with a new type of line on each of the other colored strips of paper.
4. Glue the paper onto the 18 x 6–inch black paper, leaving a small space between each colored piece of paper so that the black paper shows between each strip.

Variations

1. *Quilt with Lines:* Use squares or triangles of colored paper to create a quilt. Fill each shape with a different kind of line.
2. *Line Abstract #1:* On 18 x 6–inch heavy white drawing paper, draw five or six diagonal lines from one side of the paper to the other. The lines should be fairly evenly spaced. Draw a different type of curved or angled line in each space. Use thinned-out watercolors to paint each area a different color.

Quilt with Lines

Line Abstract #1

Line Abstract #2

3. *Line Abstract #2:* Give each student three pieces of 3 x 6–inch construction paper in a variety of colors. Using a ruler or a straight edge and a fine-point black marker, draw horizontal lines from one edge of the paper to the other, varying the distance between the lines. Fill each space with a different type of angle line or curved line. Glue the three pieces to a piece of 7 x 11–inch black construction paper.

Contour Lines

A Color of His Own

Written and illustrated by

Leo Lionni

(New York: Pantheon Books, 1975)

A young chameleon is concerned that he does not have his own color until he meets an older and wiser chameleon to share his color changes with.

How the Artist Used the Element

To create the shapes of the chameleon, the other animals, leaves, and grasses, the artist first had to draw the outlines or contours of each. After the contour line was drawn, he could color or paint what he had drawn. Contour lines are easy to find in coloring books and comic strips.

Art Exploration: Contours of Familiar Objects

Students practice drawing contour lines of familiar objects in the classroom.

Materials

- 8^1/$_2$ x 11–inch white photocopy paper
- Drawing pencils
- Erasers

Directions

1. Students select a small object from the room to draw, such as a pencil, water bottle, glue bottle, or compass.
2. Before drawing it, examine it by looking at it from all directions and feeling the outside edges of its shape.
3. Students silently describe to themselves the different lines and shapes that make up the object. For example, a pencil is two straight parallel lines with an angle line on one end and a curved line on the other end.
4. Draw the contour (outline) of the object lightly in pencil several times, each time placing the object in a different position. Do not draw any inside details.

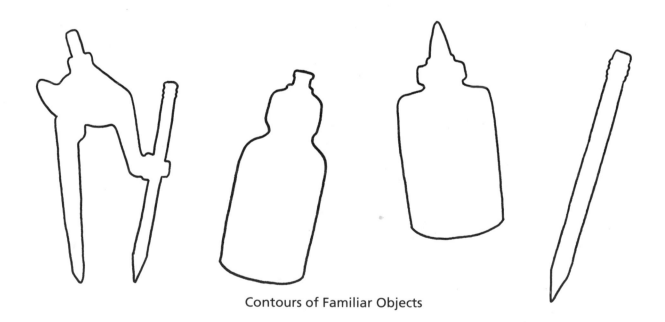

Contours of Familiar Objects

Variations

1. *Contour Ripples:* Choose a favorite contour drawing from the exploration above, or cut out a picture from a magazine or catalog. Draw (or glue) it in the center of a large piece of light-colored paper. With a marker or crayon, draw a line that follows the shape but does not trace the contour line. Repeat with different colors of markers until the paper is filled.

Contour Ripples

2. *Contour Tracing:* Cut out pictures from magazines or newspapers and trace only the contour lines (outline) of different objects, using a marker or crayon.

Contour Tracing

3. *Watercolor Animal:* On a piece of watercolor paper, lightly draw the contour of an animal such as the chameleon in *A Color of His Own.* Paint inside the shape of the animal with clean water. Before the water dries, put drops of different watercolor paint into the animal shape and watch the colors mix and spread.

Watercolor Animal

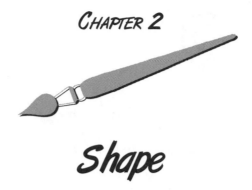

CHAPTER 2

Shape

Definitions

In a Nutshell

Shapes can be two- or three-dimensional. Two-dimensional shapes have only height and width. They are created when the ending point of a line connects to the beginning point of the same line. Three-dimensional shapes have height, width, and depth.

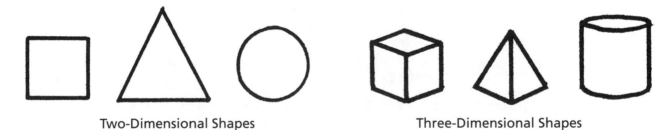

Two-Dimensional Shapes   Three-Dimensional Shapes

Taking a Closer Look

Shapes can be familiar and easy to recognize, such as squares, triangles, circles, cubes, pyramids, and cylinders. They can also be unfamiliar, irregular, and difficult to describe.

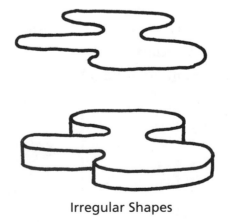

Irregular Shapes

Shapes can be created by the contour line or outline of an object.

Shapes Created by Contour Line

Or shapes can be created without a contour line or outline by using color, texture, or even a series of smaller shapes.

Shapes Created by Color, Texture, and a Series of Smaller Shapes

In art, we look at the shape of an object and the shape of the area surrounding the object. The object is the positive shape, and the shape of the space surrounding it is the negative shape. Both the shape of the object and the shape surrounding it should be considered in creating a balanced work of art.

Positive and Negative Shapes

Sculpture and architecture are easy to recognize as having three dimensions because they exist in three-dimensional space. Drawings and paintings, however, have only two dimensions—height and width. To create the illusion of three-dimensional forms on a two-dimensional surface, artists use elements of perspective. For example, parallel lines meet at a vanishing point, and a light source creates shadows and shading on a three-dimensional shape. (See the definition of space in Chapter 6.)

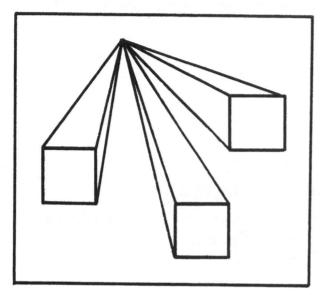

Parallel Lines Meet at Vanishing Point

Light Creates Shadows and Shading on a Three-Dimensional Shape

Fine Art Examples

Two-Dimensional Shapes

Paul Klee: *Red Balloon, Seneci,* and *Blossoming*

Pablo Picasso: *Guernica, First Steps,* and *Three Musicians*

Georgia O'Keeffe: *Evening Star*

Henri Matisse: *The Parakeet and the Mermaid* and any of his paper cutout paintings

Three-Dimensional Shapes

Claude Monet: *Haystacks, End of Summer, Morning* (one painting)

Paul Cézanne: Still life paintings

M. C. Escher: Landscape drawings and etchings

Children's Literature Examples

Two-Dimensional Shapes

Aardema, Verna. *Why Mosquitoes Buzz in People's Ears.* Illustrated by Leo and Diane Dillon. New York: Dial Press, 1975.

Cendrars, Blaise. *Shadow.* Translated and illustrated by Marcia Brown. New York: Charles Scribner's Sons, 1982.

Lionni, Leo. *A Color of His Own.* New York: Pantheon Books, 1975.

Pelletier, David. *The Graphic Alphabet.* New York: Orchard Books, 1996.

Ringgold, Faith. *Tar Beach.* New York: Crown Publishers, 1991.

Taback, Simms. *There Was an Old Lady Who Swallowed a Fly.* New York: Viking Penguin, 1997.

Three-Dimensional Shapes

Grifalconi, Ann. *The Village of Round and Square Houses.* Boston: Little, Brown, 1986.

Van Allsburg, Chris. *Jumanji.* New York: Houghton Mifflin, 1981.

———. *The Polar Express.* Boston: Houghton Mifflin, 1985.

Explorations

Tar Beach
Written and illustrated by Faith Ringgold
(New York: Crown Publishers, 1991)

A young girl living in a Harlem apartment with her parents and brother dreams of flying over the city at night. She imagines claiming everything she sees for herself and her family.

How the Artist Used the Element

The artist has created a number of wonderful views of the city at night. Notice the different shapes she used—squares and rectangles for buildings and windows; circles for lights, stars, and dishes; triangles for a quilt; rectangles for blankets; and ovals for a rug. *Optional:* Notice the horizontal, vertical, diagonal, curved, and angled lines on the bridge and girders.

Art Exploration: City at Night

Students explore rectangles, squares, and circles while creating a night cityscape.

Materials

- 12 x 18–inch dark blue construction paper
- Construction paper in a variety of colors cut into rectangles of different sizes
- Glue
- Crayons
- White, gray, and black tempera paints
- Stiff cardboard cut into $1/4$ x 3–inch strips
- Small paintbrushes
- 3 x 6–inch pieces of white paper

Directions

1. Arrange different colors and sizes of rectangles on the blue paper to create a cityscape. Orient the paper horizontally or vertically, and place building rectangles side by side or overlapping. Shapes in front should touch the bottom edge of the paper.
2. After creating a pleasing arrangement, glue the rectangles down.
3. To paint windows, dip the narrow end of the cardboard strip into paint and drag it to create rectangles and squares for the windows. Add chimneys, pipes, smaller buildings on top of larger buildings, fire escapes, and so on—anything you might see on a building. Examine the illustrations in *Tar Beach* for ideas.
4. Add small dots for stars, using white paint and the wrong end of a small paintbrush.
5. Create small self-portraits to fly over the city by using crayons and the 3 x 6–inch piece of white paper. Outline the figure with a black crayon and color it. Cut it out and glue it to the night sky.

City at Night

Variations

1. *City at Night Mural:* Give each student a choice of one large color rectangle (10 x 8 inches or 12 x 6 inches) to create one building. Glue pipes and smaller buildings on top and add windows and fire escapes. (Windows could be printed on buildings using squares and rectangles cut from potatoes or sponges.) Glue buildings along the bottom edge of a long sheet of blue or black bulletin board paper to make a cityscape for the whole classroom. Add stars and small flying self-portraits.

City at Night Mural

2. *Quilt Border:* Create a quilt border, as Faith Ringgold did, for the night cityscape by adding different-colored squares of construction paper around the edges.

Quilt Border

3. *Shapes Quilt:* Create quilts by cutting 8-inch squares of construction or wrapping paper in half and then in half again (for four squares). Cut two squares in half to make rectangles and two in half diagonally to make triangles. Glue the shapes to another piece of paper to make a quilt.

Shapes Quilt

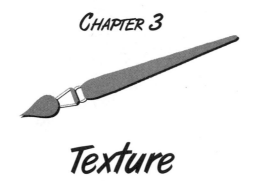

CHAPTER 3

Texture

Definitions

In a Nutshell

Texture refers to the appearance of the surface of something in a drawing or painting. Texture gives us a visual impression of how a surface would feel if we could actually touch it. It can look smooth, rough, hard, or soft. In books, the texture must be implied, because reproductions of illustrations or paintings actually feel smooth.

Taking a Closer Look

Texture is easy to explain and understand when it can actually be felt on sculptures, acrylic and oil paintings, paper cutout illustrations, and collages. However, texture must be implied in paintings and drawings printed in books because the paper on which they are printed is smooth.

Artists use lines, points, and shapes to represent different textures. Lines can be used to show the softness or roughness of fur, feathers, or hair. Points can be used to show the roughness of sandpaper or grains of salt. Shapes can be used to show the irregular surface of pebbles in a riverbed.

Fur, Feather, Hair, Salt, and Pebbles

Textures can be regular and form a pattern like scales on a fish, shingles on a house, or bricks in a wall. They can also be irregular like waves on the ocean, tousled hair, or the grain in a piece of wood.

Scales, Shingles, Bricks, Waves, Wood

Fine Art Examples

George Catlin: Paintings and drawings

John Singleton Copley: Colonial portraits

Pablo Picasso: Collages, pen-and-ink drawings, and etchings

John James Audubon: Animal paintings

Children's Literature Examples

Aardema, Verna. *Why Mosquitoes Buzz in People's Ears.* Illustrated by Leo and Diane Dillon. New York: Dial Press, 1975.

Bunting, Eve. *Smoky Night.* Illustrated by David Diaz. San Diego: Harcourt Brace, 1994.

Hodges, Margaret. *Saint George and the Dragon.* Illustrated by Trina Schart Hyman. Boston: Little, Brown, 1984.

Sendak, Maurice. *Where the Wild Things Are.* New York: Harper and Row, 1963.

Stevens, Janet. *The Three Billy Goats Gruff.* San Diego: Harcourt Brace Jovanovich, 1987.

Explorations

Where the Wild Things Are
Written and illustrated by Maurice Sendak
(New York: Harper and Row, 1963)

Sent to his room for misbehaving, a young boy imagines sailing away to an island of huge monsters who make him their king because they love him. He sails home to find the person who loves him best of all.

How the Artist Used the Element

The artist has created a wide variety of textures for the various monsters. Notice the hair and scales on the sea monster as well as the different furs, hair, and tails of the land monsters. He created all these textures by using different lines with an ink pen or small paintbrush.

Art Exploration: Monster!

Students create their own monsters.

Materials

- 9 x 12–inch good drawing paper
- Pencils
- Extra-fine-point permanent markers
- Markers, colored pencils, or crayons

Directions

1. Guide students through a simple pencil drawing of a monster. Encourage them to draw lightly. Begin with a large oval for the body. (See "Step-by-Step Directions for Drawing a Monster" on page 30.)
2. Draw a face on the oval near the top.
3. Add arms and legs by drawing two sets of curved lines for each.
4. Add hands and feet.
5. Using the extra-fine-point permanent marker, add hair, scales, fur, horns, tails, and so forth. Use different textures for different body parts. Be imaginative like Maurice Sendak. Erase the pencil lines.
6. Add a background of grass, trees, plants, and clouds.
7. Color with markers, colored pencils, or crayons.

Monster!

Step-by-Step Directions for Drawing a Monster

Variations

1. *Texture Rubbings:* Give each student a sheet of white copy paper and unwrapped, broken crayons. Fill the paper with crayon rubbings of textures from around the room (walls, floors, chairs, shoe soles) or textures you provide (nylon fruit bags, bricks, rough-textured book covers, paper doilies, burlap, wood, leaves, etc.).

Texture Rubbings

2. *Texture Rubbings on Shapes:* Cut circles, squares, triangles, and rectangles from white copy paper. Using unwrapped crayons, fill each shape with texture rubbings from around the room. Encourage students to use only one to three different colors of crayons. Suggest color schemes such as warm, cool, or monochromatic. (See color terms and concepts in Chapter 5.)

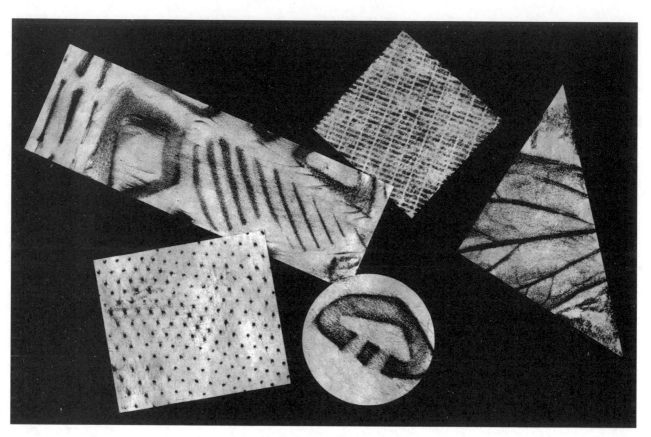

Texture Rubbings on Shapes

3. *Oil Pastel Textures:* Using a white oil pastel, draw a diagonal line on heavy drawing paper from the top edge to the bottom edge. Draw two diagonal lines from one side of the paper to the other. Fill each space with a different texture, using the oil pastel. Paint each space with watery tempera paint or watercolor. (If time permits and before starting to draw with oil pastel, tape all four sides of the paper down with masking tape. This will keep the paper from buckling when painted and will provide a thin white border.)

Oil Pastel Textures

CHAPTER 4

Value

Definitions

In a Nutshell

Value refers to the amount of light and dark in a work of art. Black is the darkest value and white is the lightest value. There is a wide array of grays between the two.

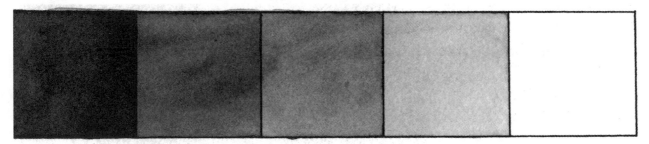

Value Scale

Taking a Closer Look

Value is an important concept in art for several reasons. It provides contrast and balance, it can make some parts of a painting or drawing appear more important than others, and it helps create the illusion of three-dimensional forms on a flat surface. By adding shading (or increasing degrees of darkness) to a flat shape such as a circle, the illusion of a sphere can be created.

Circle and Sphere

The concept of value is not limited to blacks, grays, and whites. Color also has value. A light-valued painting has a lot of light colors (see *Starry Messenger* by Peter Sis). A dark-valued painting has a lot of dark colors (see *The Polar Express* by Chris Van Allsburg). Most good paintings have a combination of light and dark values to add interest and contrast.

Fine Art Examples

Raphaelle Peale: *After the Bath*
Mary Cassatt: Value studies
Rembrandt, and Jan Vermeer: Paintings, drawings, and etchings

Children's Literature Examples

Bartone, Elisa. *Peppe the Lamplighter.* Illustrated by Ted Lewin. New York: Lothrop, Lee & Shepard Books, 1993. (Dark values)

Cendrars, Blaise. *Shadow.* Translated and illustrated by Marcia Brown. New York: Charles Scribner's Sons, 1982. (Shadows)

Grifalconi, Ann. *The Village of Round and Square Houses.* Boston: Little, Brown, 1986. (Shading and shadows)

Pilkey, Dav. *The Paperboy.* New York: Orchard Books, 1996. (Dark values)

Say, Allen. *Grandfather's Journey.* New York: Houghton Mifflin, 1993. (Sunrise on page 6 [light values] and mountains on page 11 [light and dark values])

Sis, Peter. *Starry Messenger.* New York: Farrar, Straus & Giroux, 1996. (Light values)

Van Allsburg, Chris. *Jumanji.* New York: Houghton Mifflin, 1981. (Shading and shadows)

———. *The Polar Express.* Boston: Little, Brown, 1985. (Shading and shadows)

Explorations

Value Scale

Jumanji

Written and illustrated by Chris Van Allsburg

(New York: Houghton Mifflin, 1981)

While their parents are away for the day, two bored children discover a mysterious and magical jungle adventure game that creates more excitement than the two of them could ever have imagined.

How the Artist Used the Element

Value refers to the amount of lightness and darkness in a work of art. Black is the darkest value and white is the lightest value with a wide array of grays between the two. Value provides contrast and balance, it can make some parts of a painting or drawing appear more important than others, and it helps create the illusion of three-dimensional forms on a flat surface. Notice how Van Allsburg makes his drawings appear real and three-dimensional by adding shading and shadows.

Art Exploration: Value Scale and Drawing Three-Dimensional Shapes

Students explore (1) the different colors of gray from light to dark by making a value scale and (2) how to add shading and shadows to circles, cylinders, and cubes to make them look three-dimensional.

Materials

- 9 x 12–inch white drawing paper
- Drawing pencils
- White three-dimensional shapes—ball, cylinder (salt box wrapped with white paper), box (wrapped with white paper), cone (white paper cup)
- Light source (spotlight or flashlight)

Directions for Value Scale

1. Students create a value scale to explore the different values that can be created with a pencil. Draw a long rectangle on the white paper (approximately 5 x 1 inches) and divide it into five 1-inch sections. (Or, the rectangle can be predrawn and copies made for the students.)
2. Leave the first space on the left empty, and color the second space as lightly as possible.

3. Color the third space a little darker, the fourth space darker still, and the fifth space as dark as possible.

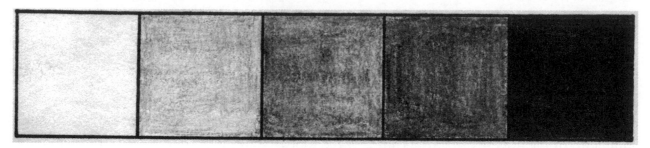

Value Scale

Directions for Drawing Three-Dimensional Shapes

1. Place the ball, cylinder, box, and cone on a table with the light shining on them from either the left or right so that shadows are created.

2. Students study and talk about what they see. (The surfaces are lightest closest to the light and darkest where they are farthest from the light. The shapes also cast shadows on the table. The shading on the ball and cylinder will gradually change from light to dark, while the shading on the box may be all one color of gray.)

3. Draw the shapes and color them with pencils to show the different colors of gray practiced on the value scale. See "Step-by-Step Directions for Drawing and Shading a Cube, Cylinder, and Cone" on page 39 if you wish to demonstrate or do a guided drawing of the different shapes.

Three-Dimensional Shapes

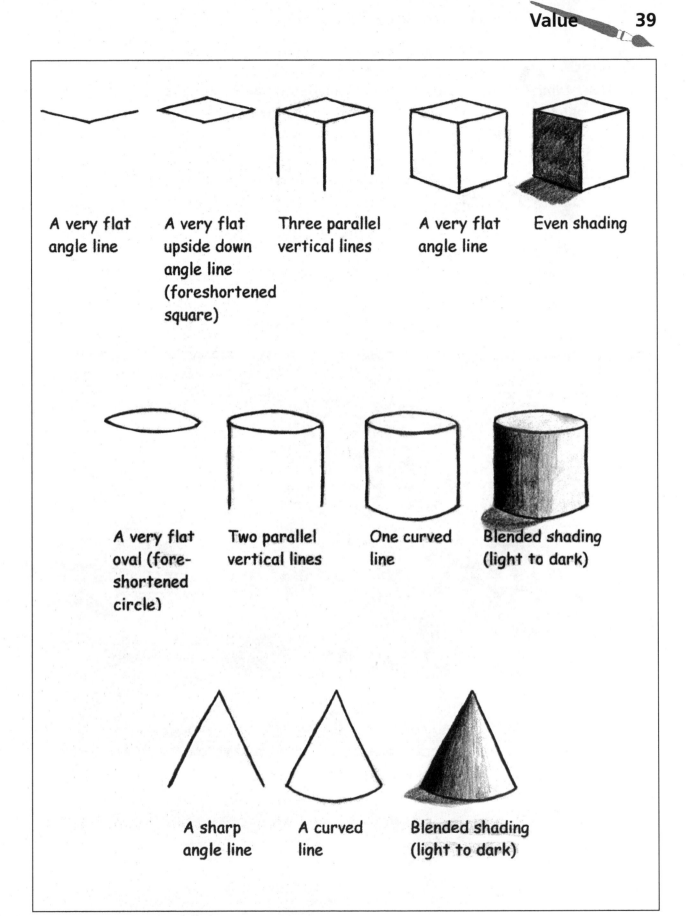

A very flat angle line

A very flat upside down angle line (foreshortened square)

Three parallel vertical lines

A very flat angle line

Even shading

A very flat oval (foreshortened circle)

Two parallel vertical lines

One curved line

Blended shading (light to dark)

A sharp angle line

A curved line

Blended shading (light to dark)

Step-by-Step Directions for Drawing and Shading a Cube, Cylinder, and Cone

Variations

1. *Three-Dimensional Shapes in Color:* Draw the three-dimensional shapes again. Use oil pastels or chalk pastels to color and shade the shapes.

2. *Black, White, and Gray Abstract:* Give each student a small amount of black and white tempera paints, a round paintbrush, a piece of heavy white paper, a paper towel, and a container of water (to keep the brush clean). Experiment mixing different quantities of black and white paints directly on the paper. See how many different colors of gray can be made.

3. *Black, White, and Gray Collage:* Cut out solid-colored gray, black, and white shapes from newspapers and magazines. Arrange the pieces in a pleasing design on a piece of white paper. Glue the shapes down.

Black, White, and Gray Abstract

Black, White, and Gray Collage

Shading and Shadows

The Village of Round and Square Houses

Written and illustrated by Ann Grifalconi

(Boston: Little, Brown, 1986)

A grandmother explains to her granddaughter why the women in their village live in round houses and the men in square ones. This book is based on a true story.

How the Artist Used the Element

In color illustrations, artists use darker colors to show the shady side of something as well as to show the shadows that are cast. They use light colors to show which side the light is shining on. Notice how the light is shining on the round and square houses on the side closest to the sun or moon, how parts of the houses are shaded on the side opposite to the sun or moon, and how the houses cast shadows.

Art Exploration: African Village

Students use chalk pastels to draw and shade round and square houses.

Materials

- 9 x 12–inch white drawing paper
- Drawing pencils
- Chalk pastels in a variety of colors
- Paper towels to rest hands on while drawing and coloring

Directions

1. With drawing pencils, lightly draw a round house and a square house.
2. Add background details, such as mountains, trees, and clouds.
3. Color the drawing with chalk pastels. Color the sides of the houses closest to the sun with a very light color. Color the sides of the houses on the farthest side from the sun a dark color. Remember to add shadows.

African Village

Variations

1. *Shadow Tracing:* On the playground or sidewalk, use chalk to outline a child's feet and his or her shadow. Trace the same child's shadow at different times throughout the day, making sure he or she always stands in the same place.

2. *Bird Shadow:* Cut a large bird or butterfly out of a light-colored piece of cardboard. Hang it in a sunny window. Tape a large piece of paper on the floor where the animal's or insect's shadow hits. Trace the animal or insect at different times of the day.

3. *Animal Shadows:* Read *Shadow* by Blaise Cendrars. Put one 6 x 6–inch piece of light-colored construction paper together with one piece of black construction paper, and staple them together at the corners. With a pencil, draw the contour (outline) of an animal or insect, such as a spider, lizard, scorpion, or caterpillar. The figure should fill the paper. Cut through both pieces of paper on the pencil line. Cut out shapes of leaves and a large rock. Glue them to a 9 x 12–inch piece of yellow, red, or orange construction paper. Glue the black shadow animal or insect on first and the light-colored animal or insect on top of it so that it overlaps.

Animal Shadows

Chapter 5

Color

Definitions

In a Nutshell

Color helps to create the mood of a painting. Bright, warm colors can give a feeling of warmth, love, or enthusiasm, cool colors can give a feeling of calm or peace, whereas very dark or drab colors can give a feeling of sadness or despair.

Color is relative—how a color looks depends on the colors around it, the colors it is mixed with, and the amount of light on it.

Taking a Closer Look

To understand how artists use color, it is helpful to understand some basic color terms and concepts:

Hue: the actual color.

Local color: the actual color of an object or a place.

Value: the lightness or darkness of a color. A tint is a light value and a shade is a dark value.

Tint: a color (hue) that is lightened by adding white.

Shade: a color (hue) that is darkened by adding black.

Intensity: the degree of purity; the brightness or dullness of a color.

Primary colors: red, yellow, and blue—the three basic colors that cannot be created by mixing other colors.

Secondary colors: orange, green, and purple—colors made by mixing two primary colors.

Tertiary colors: the colors between the primary and secondary colors on a color wheel—red-orange, yellow-orange, yellow-green, blue-green, blue-violet, and red-violet.

Complementary colors: blue and orange, red and green, yellow and purple; pairs of colors opposite each other on the color wheel. Complementary colors intensify and enhance each other (orange makes blue seem bluer and cooler, whereas blue makes orange seem hotter and brighter).

Analogous colors: colors closely related in hue. They are next to each other on the color wheel.

Monochromatic colors: a color (hue) along with its shades and tints. It may also include white and black.

Warm colors: reds, oranges, and yellows; colors that give the feeling of warmth, energy, or enthusiasm.

Cool colors: blues, greens, and purples; colors that give the feeling of coolness, calm, peace, or mystery.

Fine Art Examples of Color

Paul Klee (monochromatic): *Fugue in Red* and *Crystal Gradation*

Claude Monet (complementary colors): *Impression: Sunrise; Regatta at Argenteuil;* and *La Corniche at Cap Martin, Near Menton*

Claude Monet (cool and warm colors): Many variations of *The Japanese Bridge*

Henri Matisse (primary and secondary colors): *The Parakeet and the Mermaid*

Piet Mondrian (primary colors): *Composition with Red, Yellow, and Blue*

Paul Gauguin (complementary colors): *Tahitian Landscape*

Children's Literature Examples

Pilkey, Dav. *The Paperboy.* New York: Orchard Books, 1996. (Cool colors)

Rohmann, Eric. *Time Flies.* New York: Crown Publishers, 1994. (Monochromatic)

Say, Allen. *Grandfather's Journey.* New York: Houghton Mifflin, 1993. (Monochromatic and cool colors)

Wiesner, David. *Tuesday.* New York: Clarion Books, 1991. (Cool colors)

Williams, Vera B. *A Chair for My Mother.* New York: Greenwillow Books, 1982. (Warm colors)

Young, Ed. *Seven Blind Mice.* New York: Philomel Books, 1992. (Primary and secondary colors)

Explorations

Monochromatic Color

Grandfather's Journey

Written and illustrated by Allen Say

(Boston: Houghton Mifflin, 1993)

A Japanese–American man tells the story of his grandfather's visits to the United States. When the man visits the United States, he then understands his grandfather's feelings of being torn by love for both Japan and the United States, two very different countries.

How the Artist Used the Element

Artists sometimes use only one color to create an illustration or painting. They use the color itself (hue), the color mixed with black (shade), and the color mixed with white (tint). Notice Grandfather's portrait on page 4. Except for the colors in the grandfather's skin, the artist used only brown, shades of brown, tints of brown, and white to create the portrait. Look at the train engine on page 7 and the factories on page 10. The artist used only black, tints of black, and white to create these illustrations.

Art Exploration: Monochromatic Abstract

Students explore mixing shades and tints of a color of their choice while creating an abstract painting.

Materials

- 12 x 18–inch white drawing paper
- Plastic egg cartons (one-half carton per student)
- Round paintbrushes
- Black, white, and either red or blue tempera paints

Directions

1. Give each student half of an egg carton. Put a small amount of the student's chosen paint in one compartment, white paint in another compartment, black in another. (Students mix the paint on their paper.)
2. Paint a large part of the paper with white paint, getting as much paint off the brush as possible. Dip (don't stir) the brush into the colored paint and paint a little over the white as well as other places on the paper. Dip into the color again and paint, getting as much paint as possible off the brush onto the paper. Dip (don't stir) the brush into the black, and paint a little on the color and on the white. Dip in black

again and paint as true a black as possible. Explore different combinations, making as many new colors as possible. Leave some areas of the paper with a true white, a true color, and a true black. Cover the entire paper with paint.

Monochromatic Abstract

Variations

1. *Monochromatic Shapes:* Give each student five 5–inch squares of heavy paper. Also give each student three colors of paint—the color of their choice plus black and white. Students add either black or white to their color choice to make five new colors. Paint each square a different color. When the squares are dry, cut out regular or irregular shapes from the painted squares. Arrange the cutouts in a pleasing design on a colored piece of construction paper. Glue the shapes down.

Monochromatic Shapes

2. *Monochromatic Collages:* Divide students into six groups. Assign each group a primary or secondary color (red, yellow, blue, orange, green, or purple). Give students magazines and catalogs and ask each group to find hues, shades, and tints of their color. Cut out the color swatches and glue them onto a piece of white paper.

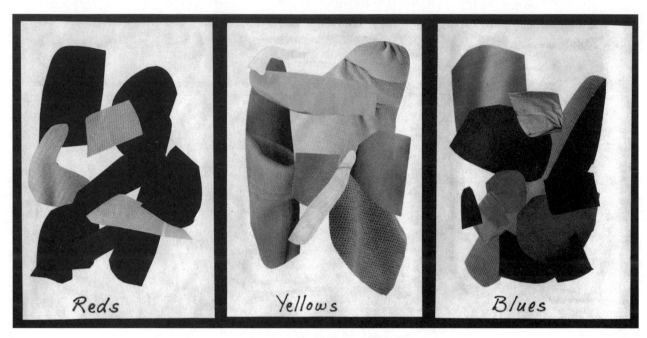

Monochromatic Collages

3. *Monochromatic Portrait:* Create a portrait like the one in *Grandfather's Journey,* using only a soft drawing pencil, black crayon, or brown, black, and white tempera paint. Ask students to explore their own faces in a mirror or to explore a partner's face. Before painting a portrait, practice drawing a face in pencil. Ask students questions such as "What shape is your head? Is it a circle, an oval, egg-shaped, or square? Where are your eyes? Are they near the top of your head or in the middle? Can you see all of the iris in each eye? Can you see white above or below the iris? What shape are your eyebrows? Do they touch in the middle? How wide is your nose? How wide is your mouth? Is your mouth closer to your chin, to your nose, or right in the middle?"

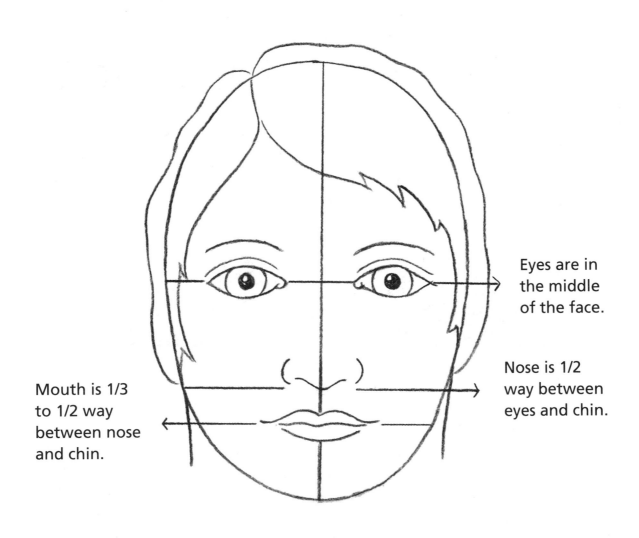

Eyes are in the middle of the face.

Nose is 1/2 way between eyes and chin.

Mouth is 1/3 to 1/2 way between nose and chin.

Landmarks of the Face

Helpful hints:

Our eyes are about one eye-width apart.

The width of our mouth is about the same as
the distance from the center of one eye to the
center of the other

The widest part of our nose is about the same
width as one of our eyes.

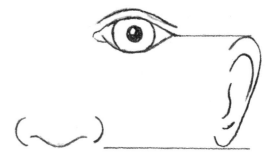

Our ears are between the middle of our eyes
and the bottom of our nose.

Pencil Portrait

Crayon Portrait

Primary and Secondary Colors

Seven Blind Mice

Written and illustrated by Ed Young

(New York: Philomel Books, 1992)

Told in verse, this story is a retelling of an East Indian fable. Seven blind mice explore different parts of an elephant and argue about what the animal is.

How the Artist Used the Element

Notice that the artist used only primary and secondary colors plus gray to paint the seven mice. (It is not necessary to explain how secondary colors are made; simply name the colors and allow the children to explore the color mixing when they begin to work.) Also notice the textures the artist used for the different parts of the elephant.

Art Exploration: Play Dough Bug

Students explore mixing red, yellow, and blue play dough to create secondary colors and then create a bug with the play dough.

Tempera Paint Portrait

Materials

- Play dough in red, yellow, and blue. (Mix 1 cup flour, $1/4$ cup salt, and 1 teaspoon cream of tartar; mix together and add 1 cup water, 1 teaspoon food coloring, and 1 tablespoon oil; cook and stir over medium heat until a "globby" mess forms; knead on lightly floured surface; store in airtight containers.)
- White copy paper folded into quarters

Directions

1. Give each student a small ball of each of the three colors of play dough. Ask students to break each ball in half and then in half again—four pieces of each color, twelve pieces in all.

2. Ask students to mix together one red and one yellow ball until no red or yellow can be seen. Discuss the new color. Repeat with one red and one blue ball. Discuss the new color. Repeat with one yellow and one blue ball. Discuss the new color. Ask students to combine the remaining two blue balls together to form one blue ball. Repeat with the two red balls to form one red ball. Repeat with the two yellow balls to form one yellow ball. Students should have six balls—one of each primary color and one of each secondary color.

3. Use the play dough to create a bug on the folded paper. Roll a big ball for the body and a smaller one for the head. Roll snakes to make legs, antennae, and stripes. Roll tiny balls to make eyes and spots. Roll egg shapes and flatten them to make wings.

Variations

Examples of some of the color explorations are not provided because black-and-white reproductions cannot do justice to these color activities. At first glance the following variations may seem repetitive. However, the key is exploration by the students.

In "Primary and Secondary Colors Abstract," students explore mixing primary colors directly on paper. Some may end up with nothing but a solid brown or gray paper. Provide students with several pieces of clean paper with the goal of seeing how many different colors they can create.

In "Color Wheel," students have greater control over their mixing as they mix colors in separate compartments in a plastic egg carton. They can see what a brushful of each new color looks like on white paper and then paint a color wheel.

In "Original Painting," students use what they have learned about color mixing to create an original painting starting with only the three primary colors and mixing the colors they need.

1. *Primary and Secondary Colors Abstract:* Give each student a piece of heavy white paper; a round paintbrush; a container of water; a paper towel; and small amounts of red, yellow, and blue paint in half of a plastic egg carton. Explore mixing combinations of two colors of paint directly on the paper. Use the water and paper towel to keep brushes clean while working. (Example not provided.)

2. *Color Wheel:* Give each student a whole egg carton, a container of water, paper, and a paintbrush. Put a small amount of red tempera paint in one end of the carton, a small amount of yellow in the middle, and a small amount of blue in the other end. Explore mixing new colors of paint in the different compartments. Copy (and enlarge if desired) the color wheel on heavy paper. Students paint the color wheel using their original primary colors and the secondary and tertiary colors they created.

3. *Original Painting:* Follow the directions for "Color Wheel." Students use their newly created colors in an original painting.

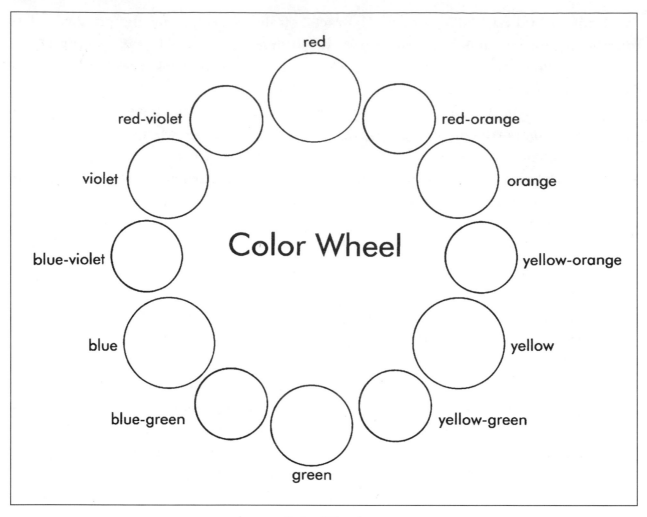

Color Wheel

Cool Colors

The Paperboy

Written and illustrated by Dav Pilkey

(New York: Orchard Books, 1996)

A young boy and his dog deliver newspapers in the cool and quiet early morning.

How the Artist Used the Element

The artist used primarily cool colors to create the illustrations—blues, greens, and purples. Even the reds and oranges are cooled down by the addition of a cool color so that they are not true red and orange hues. Notice how the use of cool colors creates the feeling of a dark and chilly early morning.

Art Exploration: Neighborhood at Night

Students create a night scene of their home or neighborhood, using only blue, green, and purple paint.

Materials

- Heavy white paper
- Round paintbrushes
- Water
- Paper towels
- Blue, green, and purple tempera paints

Directions

1. Give groups of students small containers of water and blue, green, and purple tempera paints.
2. Give each student paper, paintbrushes, and a paper towel.
3. Using only cool colors, paint a picture of your house or neighborhood. Mix the paint right on the paper. Clean the brushes often with the water and paper towels.

Neighborhood at Night

Variations

1. *Night and Day:* Fold a 12 x 18–inch sheet of heavy paper in half. Create two versions of the same painting on both halves of the paper, except use only cool colors (blue, green, and purple plus black and white) on one painting and only warm colors (red, orange, and yellow plus black and white) on the other. Compare the feelings evoked by the two paintings.

2. *Warm and Cool Paintings:* Ask half of the class to create a painting using only cool colors while the other half creates a painting using only warm colors. Compare the feelings evoked by the different color schemes.

3. *Warm or Cool Abstract:* Give students small amounts of paint in cool colors plus black and white (or warm colors plus black and white) to create an abstract painting. Mix the colors directly on the paper.

Night and Day

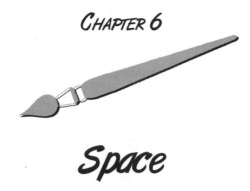

CHAPTER 6

Space

Definitions

In a Nutshell

Space in art can mean different things. It can mean the illusion of three dimensions created by using elements of perspective, or it can mean the area on the paper or canvas that separates one object or subject from another.

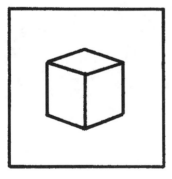

Illusion of Height,
Width, and Depth

Positive Space

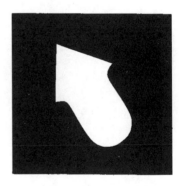

Negative Space

Foreground, Midground, and Background

Taking a Closer Look

To create the illusion of space or three dimensions on a two-dimensional surface, artists:

1. Overlap objects so that one object appears closer than another.
2. Show close-in objects larger, and faraway objects smaller.

Top triangle appears closer

3. Show close-in objects lower on the page, and faraway objects higher.
4. Show close-in objects with stronger colors and more detail, and faraway objects with lighter colors and less detail.

Close-in objects are larger, lower on the page, and more detailed, whereas faraway objects are smaller, higher on the page, and less detailed.

Three-dimensional objects cast shadows

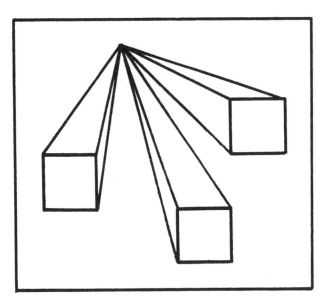

Parallel lines meet at vanishing point

5. Show parallel lines as converging and meeting at eye level.
6. Use shading and shadows to create three-dimensional forms.

In addition to referring to the illusion of three dimensions, space can refer to the area around objects. We can think of the main objects in a painting as occupying positive space (often it is the foreground). The space surrounding the object is the negative space (often it is the background). For example, in *Mirette on the High Wire* by Emily Arnold McCully, Mirette creates the positive space and everything around her is the negative space.

Fine Art Examples

Georgia O'Keeffe (positive and negative space): *Pelvis with Moon, Pelvis III,* and *Ladder to the Moon*

Paul Cézanne (overlapping shapes, shading, and shadows): Still life paintings

Georgia O'Keeffe, Paul Gauguin, Pieter Bruegel, Vincent van Gogh, Thomas Cole, Washington Allston (foreground, midground, background): Landscape paintings

M. C. Escher: Tessellation drawings and paintings

Children's Literature Examples

Aardema, Verna. *Why Mosquitoes Buzz in People's Ears.* New York: Dial Press, 1975. (Overlapping shapes)

Lester, Julius. *John Henry.* Illustrated by Jerry Pinkney. New York: Dial Books, 1994. (Foreground, midground, and background)

McCully, Emily Arnold. *Mirette on the High Wire.* New York: G. P. Putnam's Sons, 1992. (Foreground, midground, and ground)

Pelletier, David. *The Graphic Alphabet.* New York: Orchard Books, 1996. (Positive and negative space)

Van Allsburg, Chris. *Jumanji.* New York: Houghton Mifflin, 1981. (Three-dimensional space)

Wiesner, David. *Tuesday.* New York: Clarion Books, 1991. (Size and placement on the page—high or low)

Yolen, Jane. *Owl Moon.* Illustrated by John Schoenherr. New York: Philomel Books, 1987. (Positive and negative space)

Explorations

Overlapping

Why Mosquitoes Buzz in People's Ears
Written and illustrated by Verna Aardema
(New York: Dial Press, 1975)

Mosquito's annoying habit of exaggerating events starts a chain reaction that ends in disaster.

How the Artist Used the Element

Notice how the artist has overlapped the various plants and animals in the illustrations to create the illusion of three-dimensional space. The objects or animals in front look closer than the objects and animals they overlap.

Art Exploration: Jungle Scene
Students create a jungle scene by drawing overlapping plants and animals.

Materials
- White photocopy paper
- Pencils
- 12 x 18–inch white drawing paper
- Off-white oil pastels
- Round paintbrushes
- Watercolor paints
- Container of water and a paper towel for each student

Directions
1. Students select one of the animals from the book to draw—iguana, python, rabbit, crow, monkey, owl, or lion. Practice drawing the animal in pencil on the photocopy paper. Add textures.
2. With the oil pastel, draw the animal again on the drawing paper. Include textures.
3. Draw bushes, trees, other plants, and so on, behind the animal so that the animal looks as if it is in front of everything else.
4. Paint with thinned-out watercolors.

Jungle Scene

Variations

1. *Overlapping Shapes:* Give each student seven precut geometric shapes (e.g., squares, rectangles, circles, triangles) and a sheet of construction paper. With six of the shapes, create a design in which each shape overlaps or is overlapped by another shape. For contrast, place the seventh piece where it is not overlapping or touching any other piece.

2. *Overlapping Objects Collage:* Students select one category of objects to cut out of magazines and newspapers, such as shoes, lamps, cars, houses, or people. Arrange the cutout objects in order of size. Glue the objects to a large piece of paper, starting with the smallest object at the top of the paper. Glue the next largest object, overlapping the first. Continue to the bottom of the paper so that the largest cutout is at the bottom of the paper.

Overlapping Shapes

Overlapping Objects Collage

3. *Twisted Snakes:* Using pencil, draw three or four overlapping snakes on 9 x 12–inch drawing paper. Snakes should be $1/2$ to $3/4$ inch wide to allow room for designs. Trace over the snakes with a fine-point permanent marker and then color.

Twisted Snakes

Positive and Negative Space

Owl Moon

Written by Jane Yolen and illustrated by John Schoenherr

(New York: Philomel Books, 1987)

By the light of a full moon in winter, a father and daughter take a walk in the woods to see a Great Horned Owl.

How the Artist Used the Element

The front and back covers of the book provide two wonderful examples of positive and negative space. The moon, father, and daughter create the positive space while everything around them is negative space. On the back cover are the dark outlines of trees in winter. The trees create positive space while the sky in the background creates negative space. Notice the interesting negative shapes formed by the sky between the branches.

Art Exploration: Winter Tree

Students explore positive and negative space by drawing a leafless tree and filling the background spaces with color.

Materials

- 9 x 12–inch black construction paper
- White or yellow pencil or crayon
- Chalk pastels
- Examples of trees without leaves—real ones outside, a branch "planted" in a container of sand, or photographs

Directions

1. Using the pencil or crayon, draw the contour of the tree on the black paper. Allow the branches to extend beyond the edges of the paper.
2. Using either three cool or three warm colors of pastels, color the sky between the branches.

Winter Tree

Variations

1. *Tree with Textured Space:* Using a crayon or marker on white paper, draw the contour of a tree. Allow the branches to extend beyond the edges of the paper. Color the tree in a solid color. Fill the negative spaces with different textures.

Tree with Textured Space

2. *Negative and Positive Cutouts:* Fold a 6 x 9–inch piece of colored construction paper in half lengthwise. Cut out shapes from the folded edge. Glue both the 6 x 9–inch paper and the cutouts to another piece of colored construction paper.

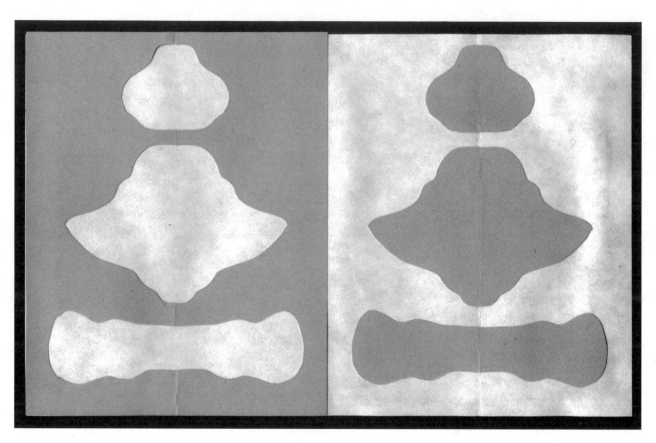

Negative and Positive Cutouts

3. *Keys:* Give each student three keys to place in a pleasing arrangement. The keys may touch or overlap. Give each student a small, 3–inch–square frame to place over the arrangement so that whole keys cannot be seen. (To make a frame, fold a 3–inch paper square in half. Starting at the folded edge, cut out a rectangle. Open up the paper and use it as a frame.) Draw the contours (outline the shape) of only what can be seen within the frame. Leave the keys white and fill in the background with textures or solid colors.

Keys

Part 2

Principles of Design

The principles of design describe the ways artists use and arrange the elements of art to create a work of art. They include, but are not limited to, harmony, variety and contrast, movement, balance, and dominance.

The following chapters each introduce a design principle to help your students understand the concept. However, a good work of art often contains more than one of the formal principles.

CHAPTER 7

Harmony

Definitions

In a Nutshell

A work of art has harmony when the art elements are organized in a pleasing way—the whole is greater than the sum of its parts. Harmony is the result of the repetition and rhythm of the various art elements used.

Taking a Closer Look

Artists balance harmony and variety to create an interesting work of art. Too much harmony may be boring or monotonous, while too much variety may be confusing or chaotic.

Harmony is achieved through the use of repetition and rhythm:

Repetition: using the same or similar things (objects, shapes, lines, colors, textures) over and over again. Look at *There Was an Old Lady Who Swallowed a Fly* by Simms Taback to see repetition of flowers, insects, and birds.

Rhythm: using the same or similar things over and over again in an order or pattern. Look at the back cover of *There Was an Old Lady Who Swallowed a Fly* to see the pattern of flies.

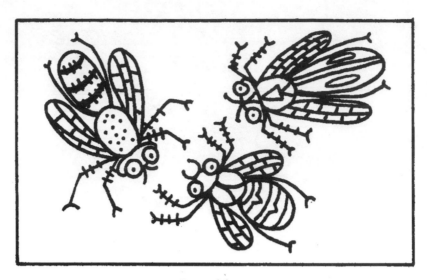

Repetition

Rhythm

Fine Art Examples

Georgia O'Keeffe (repetition of forms and colors): *Ranchos Church*

Paul Klee (repetition of straight, curved, and angled lines): *Pastorale*

Pablo Picasso (repetition of angular shapes and textures created by patterns): Cubist paintings

Andy Warhol: Soup cans and face paintings

Children's Literature Examples

Pilkey, Dav. *The Paperboy.* New York: Orchard Books, 1996. (Repetition of hills, trees, and houses)

Ringgold, Faith. *Tar Beach.* New York: Crown Publishers, 1991. (Repetition of buildings; patterns of windows)

Sis, Peter. *Starry Messenger.* New York: Farrar, Straus & Giroux, 1996. (Repetition of babies; border patterns)

Stevens, Janet. *Tops and Bottoms.* San Diego: Harcourt Brace, 1995. (Repetition of rabbits)

Taback, Simms. *There Was an Old Lady Who Swallowed a Fly.* New York: Viking Penguin, 1997. (Repetition of flowers, insects, birds, and flies)

Wiesner, David. *Tuesday.* New York: Clarion Books, 1991. (Repetition of frogs and lily pads)

Williams, Vera B. *Cherries and Cherry Pits.* New York: Greenwillow Books, 1986. (Border patterns)

Young, Ed. *Seven Blind Mice.* New York: Philomel Books, 1992. (Repetition of mice)

Explorations

Repetition

Cherries and Cherry Pits

Written and illustrated by Vera B. Williams

(New York: Greenwillow Books, 1986)

Bidemmi, a young girl, draws pictures and tells stories about her pictures as she draws.

How the Artist Used the Principle

The artist used repetition (pattern) in a wide variety of ways in this book. Notice the patterns in borders, clothing, furniture, and in the background. Even the lamp shades and rugs have patterns.

Art Exploration: Clothing Collage

Students create a collage of simple paper clothing—pants, shirts, skirts, socks, and dresses—on which they have drawn different patterns.

Materials

- 6–inch squares of white photocopy paper
- Pencils
- Scissors

- Markers in a wide variety of colors
- Glue
- 12 x 18–inch construction paper in a variety of colors

Directions

1. Using pencils, students draw the outline of different articles of clothing, such as pants, dresses, skirts, and socks, on 6–inch squares of paper. Encourage the students to make the clothing, except the socks, as long or as wide as the paper. (Clothing items could be precut for the students.)

2. Using markers, draw and color different patterns on the clothing items before cutting them out. Patterns can be created by randomly placing repeated images of objects or shapes, or by placing repeated images of objects or shapes in lines or rows.

3. Create a collage of the clothing on the large construction paper. Draw a patterned border along the edges of the construction paper.

Clothing Collage

Variations

1. *Shape Repetition:* Select one geometric shape (triangle, rectangle, square, oval, or circle). Using a black permanent marker, draw the shape ten to twenty times in different sizes and different positions on white paper. Shapes can overlap. Leave them uncolored or use only two or three different colors. See the definition of color for different color schemes, such as complementary, monochromatic, primary, or warm, in Chapter 5.

Shape Repetition

2. *Geometric Pattern:* Create a pattern using precut squares, triangles, and rectangles. The pattern can be glued to a large sheet of construction paper.

Geometric Pattern

3. *Wallpaper:* Give each student a $2^1/_8$ x $2^3/_4$–inch piece of white paper. Draw a simple object, such as a flower, water bottle, compass, stapler, or glue bottle, on the paper. Draw the object so that it fills the paper. Fold an $8^1/_2$ x 11–inch sheet of tracing paper into sixteen equal parts by folding the paper in half and then in half again. Unfold the paper. Fold it in half and then in half again in the other direction. Unfold. Trace the object in every square. Color the objects, using a specific color scheme, such as complementary, warm, cool, monochromatic, or primary. See the definition of color in Chapter 5 for more information.

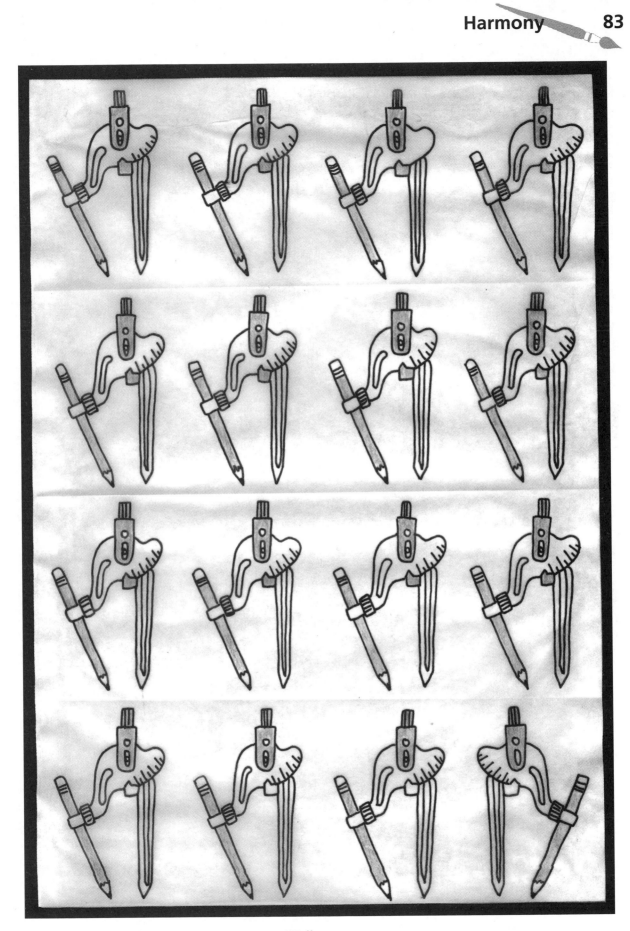

Wallpaper

Chapter 8

Variety and Contrast

Definitions

In a Nutshell

Variety makes a work of art interesting. Artists can use various sizes of objects, various colors, or various textures to add interest and excitement to their work. Contrast, or showing differences in elements or objects, is also used to make a work of art more interesting.

Taking a Closer Look

Artists balance variety and harmony to create an interesting work of art. Too much variety may be confusing or chaotic, while too much harmony may be boring or monotonous.

Variety is achieved by differences in how the elements of art are used. For example, in a line drawing, a combination of thick and thin lines may be more interesting than all thick or all thin lines.

In addition to varying the thickness of lines, artists can vary:

1. Shapes—regular and irregular
2. Position of shapes—high, low, overlapping, to the left, to the right
3. Size of shapes—small to large
4. Intensity of colors—bright to dull
5. Range of colors—a few colors to many colors
6. Textures—smooth to rough
7. Values—dark to light

Contrast is achieved by showing big differences in the elements or objects used. For example, in a design of all black squares, a red square could be added for contrast to make the work of art less monotonous. Contrast can also be used in the subject matter of a work of art—young and old, past and present, happy and sad.

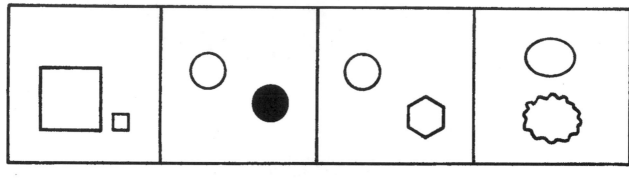

Contrasts

Fine Art Examples

Henri Matisse (variations in shapes, sizes, and positions): *The Parakeet and the Mermaid*
Henri Matisse (color contrast): *Icarus*
Winslow Homer (variety and contrast in values and in boys' bodies): *Snap the Whip*

Children's Literature Examples

Bunting, Eve. *Smoky Night.* Illustrated by David Diaz. San Diego: Harcourt Brace, 1994. (Contrasts and variations in texture)

Pilkey, Dav. *The Paperboy.* New York: Orchard Books, 1996. (Contrasts in color and value)

Say, Allen. *Grandfather's Journey.* New York: Houghton Mifflin, 1993. (Contrasts on pages 8, 11, 12, 17, 18, 22, 23, and 29)

Taback, Simms. *There Was an Old Lady Who Swallowed a Fly.* New York: Viking Penguin Books, 1997. (Variations in size, shape, color, and design of flies, birds, and flowers)

Wiesner, David. *Tuesday.* New York: Clarion Books, 1991. (Variations in shapes, sizes, and positions of frogs)

Yorinks, Arthur. *Hey, Al.* Illustrated by Richard Egielski. New York: Farrar, Straus & Giroux, 1986. (Variations in size, color, and position of birds)

Explorations

There Was an Old Lady Who Swallowed a Fly
Written by Simms Taback
(New York: Penguin Books, 1997)

A wonderfully illustrated version of the classic poem about an old woman who swallows a fly, spider, bird, cat, dog, cow, and horse.

How the Artist Used the Principle

Taback has used wonderful variety in flowers, butterflies, moths, flies, birds, dogs, grass, and much more. Notice particularly the illustration on the back cover, which is filled with different kinds of flies.

Art Exploration: Flies Everywhere!

Students create a drawing filled with flies, using a variety of shapes, sizes, and patterns.

Materials
- White photocopy paper for practice
- Pencils
- 12 x 18–inch construction paper in a variety of colors
- Extra-fine-point black permanent markers
- Colored pencils or colored markers

Directions
1. Discuss the parts of a fly. Notice the three round or oval main body parts—head, thorax, and abdomen; the two round, compound eyes; the two antennae; the six legs; and the two oval wings.

2. Guide the students through a simple drawing of a fly on the practice paper. (See "Step-by-Step Directions for Drawing Flies" on page 88.) Begin with a circle or an oval for the thorax. Draw a circle or an oval for the head, making sure it touches the thorax. Draw two circle eyes on the sides of the head so that they overlap the head. Draw a curved line for the abdomen, making sure it touches the thorax. Draw two oval wings from the thorax. Draw six legs with feet coming from the thorax.

3. Students practice drawing another fly without help. Make the legs hairy by drawing lots of short lines across the legs, and add designs to the different body parts.

4. On the large construction paper, and using the extra-fine-point marker, draw five to seven flies. Each fly should be different (shape, color, pattern, size) and should be facing in a different direction. Look at the back cover illustration for ideas.

5. Color with colored pencils or markers.

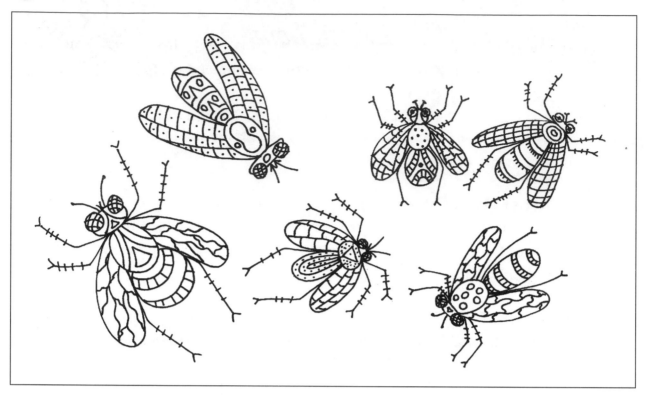

Flies Everywhere!

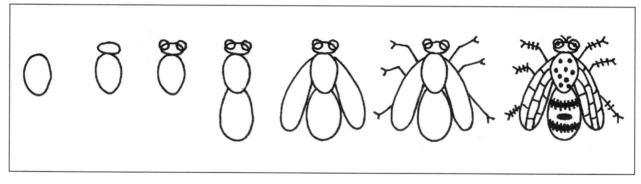

Step-by-Step Directions for Drawing Flies

Variations

1. *Butterfly with Flies:* Same as above except draw one butterfly or moth somewhere among the flies for contrast.

Butterfly with Flies

2. *Contrasting Words:* Discuss pairs of contrasting words: dark and light, big and little, tall and short, smooth and rough, fat and thin, round and pointed, and so forth. Cut 3-inch squares of white paper. On each piece of paper draw an example of a pair of contrasting words. Glue the squares to a large piece of colored construction paper. Or, as a group, glue the squares to a large sheet of bulletin board paper for a class display.

Contrasting Words

3. *Contrasts Abstract:* Using a ruler and a fine-point permanent marker, draw horizontal lines on a piece of 9 x 12–inch piece of white paper from one edge to the other. Vary the distance between the lines. In each space, make a different pattern of two contrasting shapes or lines as discussed in the definition for contrast. For example, the first space could be a pattern of red circles and white circles; the second could be a pattern of circles and squares; and so on.

Contrasts Abstract

Balance

Definitions

In a Nutshell

Balance is achieved when the art elements are arranged so that the whole work of art looks or feels stable or "balanced."

Taking a Closer Look

Balancing a work of art is like balancing two people on a teeter-totter. Two things must be considered—how big the people are and how close they are to the center. The same principles of balance are used in art. Every element or object used in a work of art has a feeling or appearance of weight. A thick line or a solid-colored shape looks heavier than a thin line or just the outline of a shape. To balance a work of art, the artist needs to consider how heavy an element or object looks, and how close it is placed to the center. All the visual elements need to be arranged so that the whole work of art looks balanced.

There are three kinds of balance in art:

Symmetry (also called formal balance): Both sides of a painting or object are identical, or very nearly so. Butterflies and human bodies are symmetrical because the left half mirrors the right half.

Asymmetry (also called informal balance): Both sides of a painting or object are different, but it "feels" balanced.

Radial Balance: A circular design with a single center. Shapes or lines radiate from a central point like petals on a daisy, spokes on a wheel, designs on a doily, or numbers on a clock.

CHAPTER 9

Symmetry

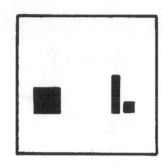

Asymmetry

Radial Balance

Fine Art Examples

Paul Klee (symmetry): *Puppet Theatre*

Georgia O'Keeffe (symmetry): *Cow's Skull: Red, White, and Blue; Open Clam Shell;* and *Closed Clam Shell*

Georgia O'Keeffe (asymmetry): *Evening Star, III*

M. C. Escher (radial balance): *Butterflies, Circle Limit III,* and *Snakes*

Children's Literature Examples

Goble, Paul. *The Girl Who Loved Wild Horses.* New York: Bradbury Press, 1978. (Radial balance on last page)

Say, Allen. *Grandfather's Journey.* New York: Houghton Mifflin, 1993. (Symmetry and asymmetry)

Sis, Peter. *Starry Messenger.* New York: Farrar, Straus & Giroux, 1996. (Radial balance and symmetry)

Yolen, Jane. *Owl Moon.* Illustrated by John Schoenherr. New York: Philomel Books, 1987. (Asymmetry)

Explorations

Radial Balance

Starry Messenger

Written and illustrated by Peter Sis

(New York: Farrar, Straus & Giroux, 1996)

The life story of Galileo Galilei, a famous Italian scientist, mathematician, astronomer, philosopher, and physicist.

Radial Design

How the Artist Used the Principle

Note the illustrations on the pages for "The Copernican System," "Galileo was amazed by what he could see with his telescope," "Hercules carrying the sky," and "Galileo was condemned." These are based on radial balance, which is a circular design with a single center.

Art Exploration: Radial Design

Students create an abstract radial design, using markers.

Materials

- 10–inch–diameter circles cut from drawing paper with a small dot to mark the center
- Markers in a variety of colors

Directions

Using the colored markers and starting in the center, draw patterns of lines and geometric shapes on paper circles, radiating out to the edge. Rotate the paper as you draw.

Variations

It would be helpful to review Chapter 4 on value before doing variations 2 and 3. For both variations, you will need scissors, a gum eraser, drawing paper, and a soft drawing pencil.

1. *Symmetrical Cut Paper Design:* Select four pieces of $8^1/_2$ x 11–inch colored construction paper. Fold one piece in half lengthwise. Starting at the folded edge, cut a wide design that goes from about 1 inch from the bottom to about 1 inch from the top of the paper. Open up the paper and glue the outside piece to a second sheet of construction paper. Fold the glued papers in half lengthwise so that the glued-on cut design is on the outside. Starting at the folded edge, cut inside the first cutout design. Open up the paper and glue it to a third sheet of paper. Fold, cut, and glue one more time as explained above.

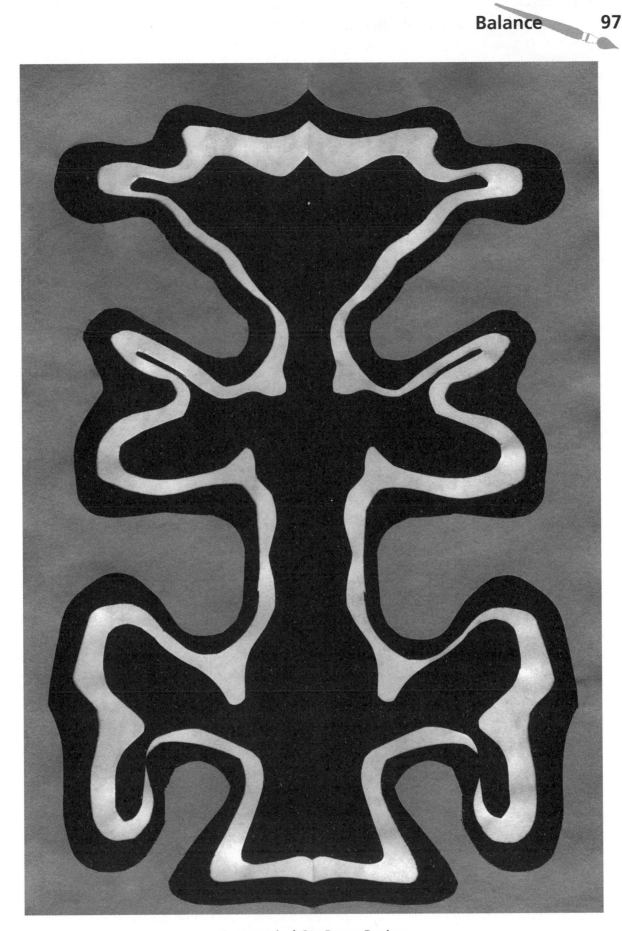

Symmetrical Cut Paper Design

2. *Symmetrical Drawing:* Find a black-and-white illustration or photograph of a person, animal, insect, or object that is symmetrical. Cut out a circle or square around the picture; do not cut on the contour line. Cut the picture in half along the line of symmetry. Glue half of it to a piece of drawing paper and draw the missing half.

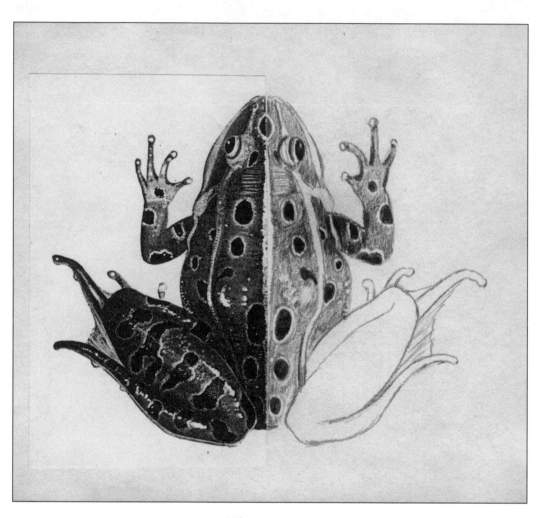

Mirror Image

3. *Mirror Image:* Find a black-and-white illustration or photograph of a person, animal, insect, or object that is asymmetrical. Cut out a circle or square around the picture; do not cut on the contour line. Cut a straight line along one side of the object in the picture so that it just touches the edges of the object. Draw a light pencil line down the middle of a piece of drawing paper and glue the object on the line. Draw the object in reverse as if it were sitting on a mirror.

Symmetrical Drawing

CHAPTER 10

Movement

Definitions

In a Nutshell

Movement in a work of art is created by the "illusion" of action.

Taking a Closer Look

Art elements can be combined to represent movement or to give the feeling of movement and action. By placing repeated elements in a work of art, the artist invites our eyes to jump rapidly or glide smoothly from one area to next.

The objects in a painting cannot actually move. However, an artist can create the "illusion" of movement or action by:

1. Repeating different objects or elements (shapes, lines, values, textures, colors) either in a regular or an irregular pattern. By repeating elements, the artist guides the viewer's eyes from one part of a work of art to another so that a feeling of movement is created.
2. Blurring the objects or elements.
3. Using "action" lines; these often used in cartoon-type drawings.
4. Placing bodies or objects a little off-balance as if caught in the middle of some action.

Fine Art Examples

John Singleton Copley: *Watson and the Shark*
Winslow Homer: *A Fair Wind (or Breezing Up)* and *The Gulf Stream*
Comic strips of superheroes in action

Children's Literature Examples

Aardema, Verna. *Why Mosquitoes Buzz in People's Ears.* Illustrated by Leo and Diane Dillon. New York: Dial Press, 1975. (Repetition of the setting sun)

Ackerman, Karen. *Song and Dance Man.* New York: Alfred A. Knopf, 1988. (Off-balance body positions and gesture lines)

Fleming, Denise. *In the Small, Small Pond.* New York: Henry Holt, 1993. (Repetition of circles around water bugs)

Goble, Paul. *The Girl Who Loved Wild Horses.* New York: Bradbury Press, New York, 1978. (Repetition of horses)

Rathmann, Peggy. *Officer Buckle and Gloria.* New York: G. P. Putnam's Sons, 1995. (Action lines and off-balance body positions)

Young, Ed. *Lon Po Po: A Red-Riding Hood Story from China.* New York: Philomel Books, 1989. (Blurred edges)

Explorations

In the Small, Small Pond
Written and illustrated by Denise Fleming
(New York: Henry Holt, 1993)

The rhyming text describes what happens to the animals in and near a small pond through spring, summer, and fall.

How the Artist Used the Principle
Notice the whirligigs and how the circles drawn around them create the feeling of the bugs moving through the water.

Art Exploration: Swimming Whirligigs
Students create a water scene of whirligigs swimming in water.

Materials

- 9 x 12–inch blue construction paper
- Fine-point black markers
- Green crayons

Directions

1. Using the black marker, students draw a small whirligig. Draw a black oval about $1/2$–inch long, and color it in solidly. Draw a small dot for the head and six curved lines for the legs.
2. Using the green crayon, draw a circle around the whirligig. Draw two or three more circles around the whirligig, with each circle getting slightly bigger to look like water ripples.
3. Continue drawing whirligigs until the paper is filled. Encourage students to have their whirligigs go in a variety of directions.

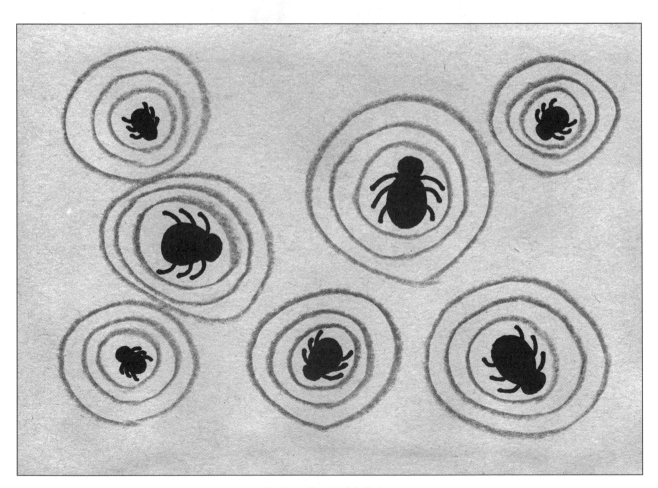

Swimming Whirligigs

Variations

1. *Action Shot:* Find or draw a picture of an animal or person in action, such as running, jumping, or diving. To use the picture for tracing, first cut broadly around the general shape of the picture; do not cut on the contour line (outline). Glue the picture to a heavy piece of paper. Carefully cut out the picture on the contour line. With a pencil or extra-fine-point marker, trace the picture eight to ten times on another piece of paper. The outlines should overlap. Glue the picture to the paper so that it overlaps the last tracing.

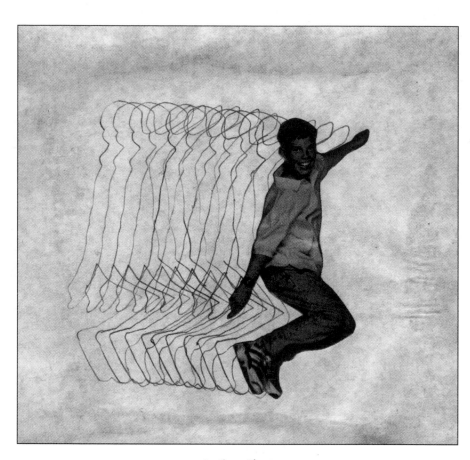

Action Shot

2. *Spinning Objects:* Step 1—On a piece of white drawing paper, draw the front, back, and side views of an object such as a car, telephone, television, shoe, airplane, or boat. All three drawings should be the same height. Step 2—On the tracing paper, trace all three views so that they overlap and give the impression of the object spinning or being seen from three sides at once.

3. *Movement Illustration:* Ask students to think about how they would show a fish swimming upstream, a tree being bent by the wind, an object falling off a table, or a leaf or piece of trash being carried by the wind. Select one of these ideas (or an original idea) to illustrate.

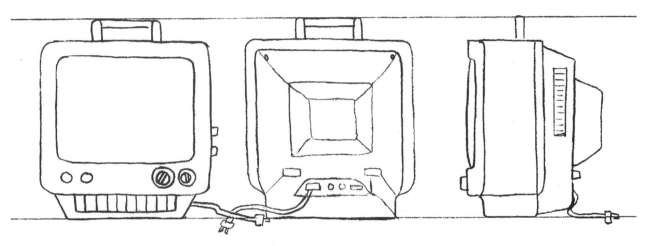

Spinning Objects: Step 1

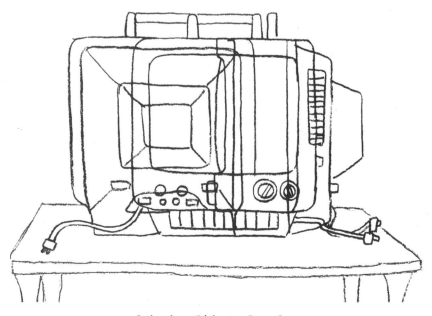

Spinning Objects: Step 2

CHAPTER 11

Dominance

Definitions

In a Nutshell

Dominance is making one object or element more important than anything else in a work of art. It is the focal point or center of interest to which our eyes keep returning.

Taking a Closer Look

A dominant area in a work of art can be created by:

1. Contrasts in size, value, color, texture, shape, and/or position of objects or elements
2. Grouping objects together
3. Something unusual or unexpected
4. Converging lines
5. Lines that direct eye movement to the focal point

A work of art without a focal point can be confusing or boring. If everything has equal importance and nothing stands out, there is nothing to draw the viewers' interest.

Fine Art Examples

Mary Cassatt (child contrasted to blue room): *The Blue Room*
Georgia O'Keeffe (size and position of subject; unusual subject): *Summer Days*
Meindert Hobbema (converging lines): *The Avenue, Middelharnis*

Children's Literature Examples

Ho, Minfong. *Hush! A Thai Lullaby.* Illustrated by Holly Meade. New York: Orchard Books, 1996.

Hodges, Margaret. *Saint George and the Dragon.* Illustrated by Trina Schart Hyman. Boston: Little, Brown, 1984.

Sis, Peter. *Starry Messenger.* New York: Farrar, Straus & Giroux. 1996.

Van Allsburg, Chris. *Jumanji.* New York: Houghton Mifflin, 1981.

Explorations

Saint George and the Dragon

Adapted by Margaret Hodges and illustrated by Trina Schart Hyman

(Boston: Little, Brown, 1984)

George, the Red Cross Knight, brings peace and happiness to the land by slaying the terrible dragon that has been terrorizing the countryside. This story is a retelling of *The Faerie Queene* by Edmund Spenser.

How the Artist Used the Principle

Every illustration should have some kind of dominance. As you explore each illustration in *Saint George and the Dragon,* try to determine what part of the illustration is dominant (the focal point) and what the artist has done to make it the center of interest. For example, on page 6, the knight is dominant because of his size and because there is an implied line drawing your eyes from the dwarf to the lamb to the princess and then to the knight. On page 15, the upper part of the dragon is dominant because of its brighter colors, its upper central location on the page, and its detailed textures. Also notice that the horse, the knight's head, and the lance all point to the dragon's upper body.

Art Exploration: Dominance Triptych

Students design a triptych (three-panel) abstract with construction paper and markers that illustrates three ways to create dominance using size, texture, and shape.

Materials

- 10 x 5–inch white paper (three per student)
- 12 x 18–inch construction paper in a variety of colors
- Construction paper in a variety of sizes and colors, cut into geometric shapes (circles, squares, triangles, rectangles)
- Glue

Directions

1. Select five to seven geometric shapes of about the same size. Select one shape that is larger.

2. On one piece of 10 x 5–inch white paper, experiment and explore different ways of creating a design with the paper shapes. Shapes can be touching each other, turned in any direction, and/or overlapping.

3. Glue the pieces down only after all the shapes are in place and a pleasing design has been created.

4. Select five to seven geometric shapes of the same color (can be different colors than used in first design). Select one shape of a different color. Repeat steps 2 and 3 above.

5. Select five to seven geometric shapes of the same shape (can be different colors than used in first two designs). Select one shape that is a different shape. Repeat steps 2 and 3 above.

6. Glue the three designs to a 12 x 18–inch piece of construction paper.

Dominance Triptych

Variations

1. *Newsprint Collage:* On a piece of 9 x 12–inch white paper, make a collage from pieces of torn newspaper. Cover the white paper completely. Cut out a colored picture, or part of a picture, from the comics section or from a magazine. Glue the colored picture down in an interesting position and place it on the black-and-white newsprint collage.

Newsprint Collage

2. *Radiating Lines Design:* With a marker, draw a dot (approximately half an inch across) somewhere on a piece of 9 x 12–inch white paper. Using a ruler, draw straight lines radiating out from the dot all the way to the edges of the paper. Radiating lines should start about a quarter inch from the dot. The spaces between the lines could be colored following a specific scheme such as monochromatic, cool, primary, or complementary. See Chapter 5 for more information.

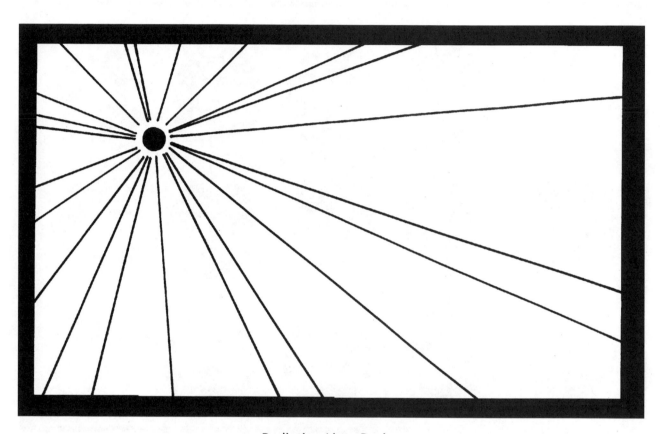

Radiating Lines Design

3. *Apple Prints:* Make a fruit print pattern, using a real apple cut in half. Make rows of apple prints with red paint. Before finishing all the rows, make one apple print in green, and then continue with the red apple prints. (Sponge shape prints could also be used, as well as different kinds of fruits and vegetables and with different color combinations.)

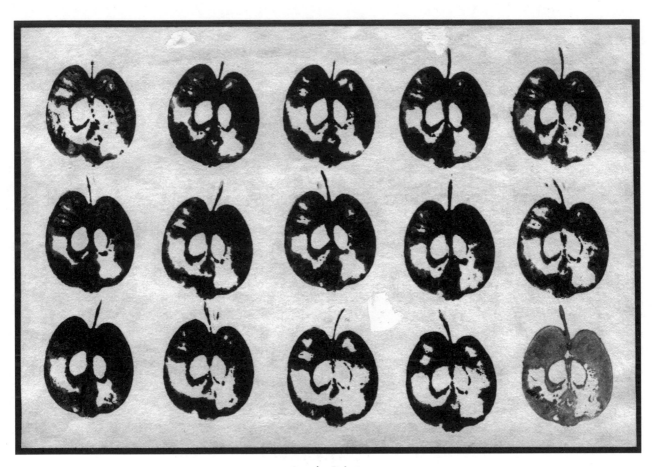

Apple Prints

Artistic Styles

Artistic styles have been changing and evolving since humans created cave paintings thousands of years ago. From those early cave paintings to the present, artistic styles have ranged from realistic to abstract. As each new generation of artists struggled for new and different ways to express themselves and the world around them, new artistic styles evolved. Art critics and art historians emerged and assigned names to artistic styles, such as realism, expressionism, and impressionism.

Many picture-book illustrators have the ability to imitate a variety of artistic styles. They understand the nuances of different styles and can create illustrations in the artistic style they feel will best tell the story. For example, Paul O. Zelinsky illustrated *Rapunzel* (New York: Dutton Children's Books, 1997) in the style of the Italian Renaissance, *Rumpelstiltskin* (New York: Dutton Children's Books, 1986) in the style of realism, and Anne Issac's *Swamp Angel* (New York: Dutton Children's Books, 1994) in the style of American naive artists.

Some of the most common historical artistic styles used by picture-book illustrators are realism, impressionism, expressionism, surrealism, naive, and cartoon. It is not always easy, or necessary, to identify a particular book's artistic style. The following chapters provide tools to recognize and appreciate some of the major categories of artistic styles that have been used by artists over the years.

Each chapter includes a short list of famous artworks created during the time the specific style was popular. It would be an interesting and valuable art history and art appreciation lesson to compare and contrast the artworks for which the artistic style was named with the picture book using that particular style.

Chapter 12

Realism

Definitions

In a Nutshell

Realism is representational art. Realists paint familiar and ordinary objects, scenes, events, and people as they truly look.

Taking a Closer Look

From the beginning of time, artists have attempted to paint realistically. But art, like everything else, goes through periods in which one style of doing things is more accepted and popular than in another period. Just prior to the 1850s, accepted and popular styles were neoclassic and romantic. Neoclassic artists tried to re-create art in the style of ancient Greece and Rome. They painted, drew, and sculpted people and scenes that represented high ideals of courage, sacrifice, and honor. Romantic artists painted a romanticized view of the world around them. They filled their paintings with scenes of unspoiled wilderness, exotic places, and faraway times.

By 1850, many artists began to reject the idea that art had to represent lofty ideals, aristocratic people, or romantic views of nature. They wanted to paint everyday, contemporary life as they saw it. Gustave Courbet, the father of nineteenth-century realism, stated, "The art of painting can consist only in the representation of objects visible and tangible to the painter" (*The Corn Sifters*, Gardner 1980, p. 758).

Characteristics of Realism

1. Ordinary people and their daily lives as subjects
2. Not necessarily photographically accurate, but a sincere and honest response of the artist to his or her everyday environment; interest in using elements of art such as space, three-dimensional shapes, and value
3. Not necessarily "pretty" or historically important subjects
4. Local color—the actual color of an object or place; realistic colors

Fine Art Examples

Gustave Courbet (French, 1819–1877): *The Corn Sifters*

Jean François Millet (French, 1814–1875): *The Gleaners*

Winslow Homer (American, 1836–1910): *Snap the Whip*

Children's Literature Examples

Steptoe, John. *Mufaro's Beautiful Daughters: An African Tale.* New York: Lothrop, Lee & Shepard Books, 1987.

Say, Allen. *Grandfather's Journey.* New York: Houghton Mifflin, 1993.

Yolen, Jane. *Owl Moon.* Illustrated by John Schoenherr. New York: Philomel Books, 1987.

Explorations

Mufaro's Beautiful Daughters
Written and illustrated by John Steptoe
(New York: Lothrop, Lee & Shepard Books, 1987)

Mufaro has two beautiful daughters, one kind and gentle, the other mean-spirited and selfish. They travel to see the king in hopes of being chosen to be his wife.

How the Artist Used the Style

The artist has illustrated the daily lives of two girls from a small village. To increase the realistic feeling, he accurately drew people, places, and animals and used realistic colors.

Art Exploration: Colored Symmetrical Drawing

Students draw and color the missing half of an illustration or photograph of a plant or animal of their choosing.

Materials

- Good drawing paper
- Pencils
- Colored pencils or watercolors, paintbrushes, and water
- Symmetrical photographs or lifelike illustrations of a variety of plants and animals

Directions

1. Show students the animal and plant illustrations in the first ten pages of the book. Notice how the artist has drawn different textures—fur, feathers, flowers, and leaves. Also notice how he has used different shades of colors—browns, greens, reds, yellows, and so on—to create more realistic illustrations.

2. Find symmetrical colored photographs or drawings of plants or animals—the left side mirrors the right side. Cut them in half down the middle. Students glue one side of the photograph or drawing to a piece of paper. Draw and color the other half, trying to match the colors and values.

Colored Symmetrical Drawing

Variations

1. *Animal Portrait:* Examine a realistic-looking stuffed animal, or use a good photograph of an animal. Begin with a careful contour (outline) drawing of the animal. Add textures, shading, and colors.

Animal Portrait and Original Photo

2. *Still Life:* Set up a still life display, using pots and baskets similar to those illustrated in the book. Use a spotlight to emphasize the light on the objects. Using a soft drawing pencil or drawing charcoal, make a careful contour drawing (outline). Add shading and shadows so that the objects look three-dimensional. (See definition of value in Chapter 4.)

Still Life

3. *Self-Portrait:* Using a soft drawing pencil and a mirror (or a fairly large photograph), draw a self-portrait. Add shading and shadows to make the portrait look three-dimensional. (See definition of value in Chapter 4.) If using a photograph, a photocopy of it will help to emphasis the values (darks and lights).

Self-Portrait and Photo

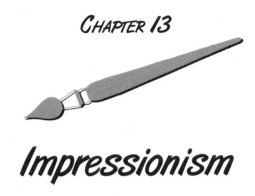

CHAPTER 13

Impressionism

Definitions

In a Nutshell

Impressionists painted their impression of a natural scene by working quickly in natural light, often outside. They used pure colors applied with short brushstrokes, and concentrated more on painting the quality of reflected light than on the objects or subjects themselves.

Taking a Closer Look

The term "impressionist" was coined by a French art critic in 1874 to describe this new way of painting. Impressionist paintings had none of the detail, traditional design, and accuracy of the paintings that preceded them. Artists concentrated on how light affects the actual color of an object. They were more interested in suggesting the shapes of objects than in painting very clear outlines of the objects.

The actual color of an object (its local color) changes as the light on it changes. A green leaf catching the rays of the morning sun may appear more yellow; at noon on an overcast day it may appear gray; and then, in the light of the setting sun, it may take on an orange or reddish hue. The impressionists wanted to capture this light and its effects on objects—"To break up the ray of light, to catch its vibrancy in the air, to follow it as it glides around objects enveloping them with color" (Courthion 1997, p. 12).

When one looks at an impressionist painting at very close range, it appears abstract. Forms and objects take shape when the artwork is viewed from a distance, allowing the eyes to blend the colors and brushstrokes into a recognizable image. Small points of pure color (often complementary colors) on the canvas cause the viewer's eyes to mix and blend colors into larger areas to suggest three-dimensional shapes.

Characteristics of Impressionism

1. Paint applied in short, rapid brushstrokes or dabs
2. Natural and informal scenes as subjects
3. Emphasis on light, reflected light, and perceived colors of the objects or subjects
4. Generally colors very light and bright
5. Objects not outlined
6. Shadows made by using complementary colors together; for example, red and green, yellow and purple, blue and orange

Fine Art Examples

Claude Monet (French, 1840–1926): *Wild Poppies, The Artist's Garden at Vetheuil, The Japanese Bridge, Water Lilies,* and *Regatta at Argenteuil*

Edgar Degas (French, 1834–1917) French: *Danseuses Basculant* and *Examen de Danse*

Mary Cassatt (American, 1844–1926) American: *Mother About to Wash Her Sleepy Child* and *Little Girl in Blue Armchair*

Children's Literature Examples

Bjork, Christina. *Linnea in Monet's Garden.* Illustrated by Lena Anderson. Stockholm: Raben & Sjögren Publishers, 1985.

Say, Allen. *Grandfather's Journey.* New York: Houghton Mifflin, 1993.

Zolotow, Charlotte. *Mr. Rabbit and the Lovely Present.* Illustrated by Maurice Sendak. New York: Harper and Row, 1962.

———. *Say It!* Illustrated by James Stevenson. New York: Greenwillow Books, 1980.

Explorations

Linnea in Monet's Garden

Written by Christina Bjork and illustrated by Lena Anderson

(Stockholm: Raben & Sjögren Publishers, 1985)

Linnea shares a love of flowers with her neighbor, Mr. Bloom. Together they travel to Paris to visit Claude Monet's garden and explore his paintings.

How the Artist Used the Style of Impressionism

Not all of Anderson's illustrations in this book are in an impressionistic style. Note the illustration on pages 20 and 21. Here Anderson approaches an impressionist style by using dabs of paint, a natural and informal scene of Linnea playing with a cat in the garden, light and bright colors, and flowers and leaves that are not outlined.

Art Exploration: Impressionist Garden

Students create an impressionist garden by dabbing tempera paints with a cotton swab.

Materials

- Cotton swabs (several for each student)
- Toothpick (one for each student)
- Tempera paints in green, blue, red, yellow, orange, and purple

Directions

1. Starting with green and yellow paints, fill in most of the garden with dabs of paint. It is all right if the colors overlap and mix.
2. Use the toothpick to drag through the wet paint to make stems.
3. Dab bright, colorful flowers on top of the green and yellow leaves.

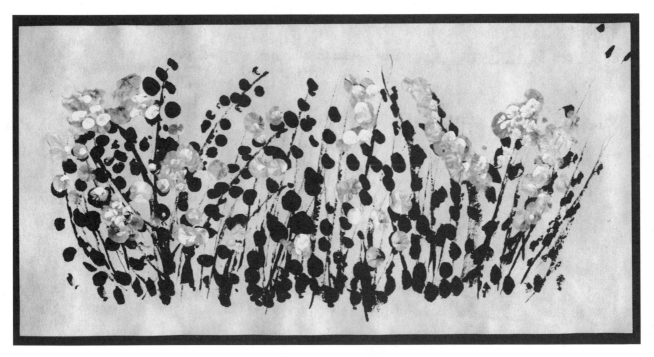

Impressionistic Garden

Variations

1. *Complementary Flowers:* Many impressionist painters used complementary pairs (red and green, blue and orange, yellow and purple) of colors in their paintings. When complementary colors are placed closed together, the colors seem to vibrate. Blue looks brighter when placed next to orange, red looks brighter when placed next to green, and yellow looks brighter when placed next to purple. Give each student red, green, blue, orange, yellow, and purple oil pastels. Make short strokes of red in a circle like the petals of a flower. Surround it with short strokes of green. Repeat using red and orange, and then red and blue. In which combination does the red look brighter? Make more "flowers," using different pairs of complementary and noncomplementary colors.

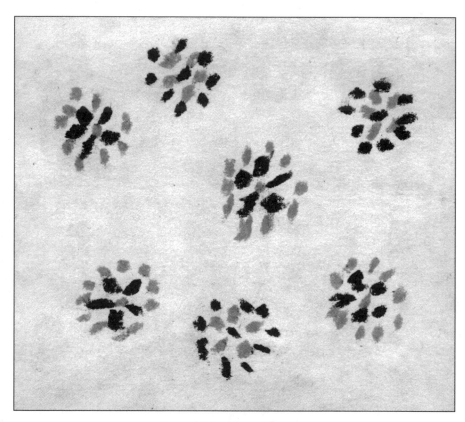

Complementary Flowers

2. *Seascape:* Many impressionist painters tried to paint the way light and objects reflect on water. This exploration takes two sessions because the paint needs to dry between sessions. On the first day, fill a sheet of heavy drawing paper with short brushstrokes of dark blue, light blue, and white tempera paints. Change colors without cleaning the brush. Make short strokes of white in the upper half for clouds. When the paint is dry, paint a small orange boat with big white sails. Make short strokes of orange and white paint below the boat for the boat's reflection on the water.

Seascape

3. *Pointillism Painting:* One of the most famous painters in the impressionist style was Georges Seurat. Many of his paintings were just dots of pure color. This style was called pointillism. Create a painting of a tropical fish or a butterfly, using tempera paints and just dots. Use the wrong end of a paintbrush to make the dots.

Pointillism Painting

Chapter 14

Expressionism

Definitions

In a Nutshell

Expressionists "express" strong emotional feelings by distorting shapes and by using strong colors, loose brushstrokes, and bold, simplified lines.

Taking a Closer Look

Throughout history, artists have expressed powerful emotions by distorting forms and using forceful colors. The term "expressionism," describing a particular style of art, evolved during the early 1900s in Germany. The primary concern of the expressionists was to create "the inner spiritual meaning of a picture rather than with its external appearance" (*Encyclopedia of Art*, 1968, p. 1537).

Expressionism rebelled against the lack of passion in the impressionistic style of art that preceded it. While impressionists were concerned with how light played on the surface of their subjects, the expressionists sought a core of reality that would make even ordinary subjects "vibrate with a living spirit" (*Encyclopedia of Art*, 1968, p. 1536).

Characteristics of Expressionism
1. Distorted shapes
2. Strong, bold colors
3. Simple, bold lines
4. Subjects of personal importance to the artist
5. Loose, expressive brushstrokes

Fine Art Examples

Edvard Munch (Norwegian, 1863–1944): *The Scream*

Vincent van Gogh (Dutch, 1853–1890): *The Starry Night*

Paul Klee (German Swiss, 1879–1940): *The Artist at the Window*

Children's Literature Examples

Bartone, Elisa. *Peppe the Lamplighter.* Illustrated by Ted Lewin. New York: Lothrop, Lee & Shepard Books, 1993.

Bunting, Eve. *Smoky Night.* Illustrated by David Diaz. San Diego: Harcourt Brace, 1994.

Williams, Sherley Anne. *Working Cotton.* Illustrated by Carole Byard. San Diego: Harcourt Brace, 1992.

Young, Ed. *Lon Po Po: A Red-Riding Hood Story from China.* New York: Philomel Books, 1989.

Explorations

Smoky Night

Written by Eve Bunting and illustrated by David Diaz

(San Diego: Harcourt Brace, 1994)

During the Los Angeles riots, a young boy and his mother learn the value of getting along with people of different nationalities and backgrounds.

How the Artist Used the Style

Notice the strong colors the artist used throughout the book—blues and purples on people's skin and thick black outlines on people, animals, and objects. Notice also that colors are not always blended together. Brushstrokes of different colors of paint are visible.

Art Exploration: Expressionist Self-Portrait

Students create a portrait of themselves expressing a strong emotion, such as happiness, excitement, fear, anger, or pain.

Materials

- Mirrors
- Pencils
- Fine-point permanent black markers
- Heavy drawing paper
- Tempera paint in a variety of colors
- Round paintbrushes

Directions

1. Students examine their own faces in the mirror as they express different emotions—happiness, excitement, pleasure, fear, anger, sadness, and so on.
2. Using a pencil, draw a self-portrait of head and shoulders only. (See information on drawing portraits in Chapter 12.)
3. Trace over the pencil lines with a marker.
4. Paint the portrait, using colors that help to show the emotion expressed. Do not paint over the black lines.

Variations

1. *Portrait of a Friend:* Follow the directions for "Expressionist Self-Portrait," except draw and paint a portrait of a friend, pet, or family member expressing a strong emotion.

Expressionist Self-Portrait

2. *Tree in a Storm:* Using expressive brushstrokes and strong colors, paint a tree on a stormy, windy day.

Tree in a Storm

3. *Expressionist Abstract:* Create an abstract painting, using strong colors and bold brushstrokes to show a mood or emotion. (See the definitions of warm and cool colors in Chapter 5.)

Expressionist Abstract

CHAPTER 15

Surrealism

Definitions

In a Nutshell

Surrealists try to paint the confusion and contradictions of mixing together the dream life (unconscious) and the wakeful life (conscious).

Taking a Closer Look

Surrealist painters combined conscious and subconscious reality into a new kind of reality—a superreality (*surréalité* in French, a term coined by the French poet André Breton).

In dreams, objects and situations repeat and change. Surrealists sometimes use multiple images to suggest the many images created in dreams. In many surrealist paintings and illustrations, unrelated and irrelevant objects are placed in unexpected situations. "The impossible landscape and its impossible contents we recognize as perfectly possible in the dream world" (Gardner 1980, p. 832).

Characteristics of Surrealism
1. Extraordinary placement of ordinary objects
2. Mixing up of ordinary situations
3. Exploring the unconscious mind and dream life
4. Great artistic freedom in choosing subjects, events, styles, and media
5. Fantastical landscapes

Fine Art Examples

René Magritte (Belgian, 1898–1967): *The Listening Room* and *Time Transfixed*

Salvador Dali (Spanish, 1904–1989): *The Persistence of Memory*

Kay Sage (American, 1898–1963): *I Saw Three Cities*

Children's Literature Examples

Barrett, Judi. *Cloudy with a Chance of Meatballs.* Illustrated by Ron Barrett. New York: Atheneum Publishers, 1978.

Van Allsburg, Chris. *Jumanji.* New York: Houghton Mifflin, 1981.

Wiesner, David. *Free Fall.* New York: Lothrop, Lee & Shepard Books, 1987.

———. *Tuesday.* New York: Clarion Books, 1991.

Explorations

Tuesday
Written and illustrated by David Wiesner
(New York: Clarion Books, 1991)

On a quiet Tuesday evening, frogs sitting on lily pads mysteriously rise into the air and glide through the nearby town while the people sleep.

How the Artist Used the Style

Frogs on lily pads are an expected and ordinary occurrence; however, frogs on lily pads floating through the night sky and through open windows are not. The realistic illustrations, combined with the floating frogs against a moonlit sky, create a dreamlike, surreal impression.

Art Exploration: Next Tuesday

Students create a picture of what happens on the next Tuesday after the frogs and pigs have flown.

Materials

- White photocopy paper
- 12 x 18–inch white drawing paper
- Pencils
- Colored pencils or markers
- Small plastic animals

Directions

1. Students select an animal to draw and examine it closely from every angle—top, bottom, front, back, and side.

2. On the photocopy paper, practice drawing the animal from a variety of viewpoints and in a variety of sizes.

3. On the drawing paper, draw the animal in a variety of sizes and from a variety of viewpoints. Overlap some of the animals.

4. Draw the tops of trees, houses, and buildings along the bottom 2 inches of the paper.

5. Color the drawing with colored pencils or markers. To create the feeling of objects floating in the sky, completely color the background in sky colors and add stars, clouds, sun and/or moon.

6. Encourage students to use the side of the colored pencil lead rather than the point itself when coloring large areas such as the sky.

Next Tuesday

Variations

1. *Invasion:* Instead of animals, draw inanimate objects, such as school supplies, fruit, cars, or furniture, floating through the sky.

Invasion

2. *Surrealist Landscape:* Cut a jagged mountain range from a piece of 9 x 12–inch dark-colored construction paper and glue it to a 9 x 12–inch piece of lighter-colored construction paper. Cut out two or three objects or people, which when added to the landscape create an impossible, "surreal" situation. Cut out trees, bushes and/or flowers to add to the realism of the landscape.

Surrealistic Landscape

3. *Surrealistic Collage:* Cut out images such as people, objects, animals, and plants from magazines. Glue them to a piece of paper to form unusual combinations.

Surrealistic Collage

CHAPTER 16

Naive Style

Definitions

In a Nutshell

Naive art refers to the work of self-taught artists who may not have had formal artistic training. Their art does not depend on any artistic traditions, such as impressionism, realism, or surrealism. Naive artists and folk artists paint subjects they know with obsessive detail. Their paintings tend to look flat rather than three-dimensional.

Taking a Closer Look

Naive artists take their art very seriously. They paint from personal experience and usually combine reality with imagination, expression, and fantasy. People and animals are often painted in stiff poses, and often with inaccurate proportions. Many of the conventions for creating perspective (three-dimensional space) are not used. Before naive art became a recognized style, it was, in its very earliest form, the purest of all the arts because it is so personally expressive.

Naive artists spend a great deal of time on minute details, such as painting every leaf on a tree and every blade of grass. They are very spontaneous in their color choices, using strong, intense colors and high contrasts.

A related style that some, but not all, sources consider to be distinct from naive art is folk art. Folk artists are trained in their cultural traditions. Their art is based on custom rather than on individual taste. Folk art is generally created to enhance the beauty of functional items, such as pottery, rugs, clothing, and toys.

Characteristics of Naive Style

1. Very personal subjects and images
2. Combination of real objects and dream world objects
3. Great attention to detail
4. Intense, nonnaturalistic color combinations
5. Stiff poses
6. Inaccurate body proportions
7. Flat, rather than three-dimensional
8. Intuitive, expressive, and spontaneous

Fine Art Examples

Henri Rousseau (French, 1844–1910): *The Snake Charmer* and *The Sleeping Gypsy*

Edward Hicks (American, 1780–1849): *The Peaceable Kingdom*

Grandma Moses (American, 1860–1961): *The Quilting Bee* and *Hoosick Falls, New York, in Winter*

Horace Pippin (American, 1888–1946): *Domino Players* and *Holy Mountain*

Children's Literature Examples

Issacs, Anne. *Swamp Angel.* Illustrated by Paul O. Zelinsky. New York: Dutton Children's Books, 1994.

Ringgold, Faith. *Tar Beach.* New York: Crown Publishers, 1991.

Taback, Simms. *There Was an Old Lady Who Swallowed a Fly.* New York: Penguin Books, 1997.

Williams, Vera B. *A Chair for My Mother.* New York: Greenwillow Books, 1982.

Explorations

A Chair for My Mother
Written and illustrated by Vera B. Williams
(New York: Greenwillow Books, 1982)

After all their belongings are destroyed by a fire, a young girl, her mother, and her grandmother save change to buy themselves a big, new, comfortable armchair.

How the Artist Used the Style

Notice the bright blues, yellows, reds, oranges, and greens the artist has used. Also notice all the wonderful little details, from the food in the bakery to the pots and pans in the kitchen to the street scene with the neighbors bringing furniture and clothing.

Art Exploration: Naive Self-Expression

Students draw and color a picture of their own choice.

Materials

- Students' choice

Directions

Children's art is naive art. The subject matter is very personal and the artwork is intuitive, expressive, and spontaneous. Asking students to create art in the naive style is an opportunity to encourage and support their natural artistic expression. Allow them to choose their own subject matter, colors, and materials. Give them the time and opportunity to share with others what they have created.

Variations

1. *My Home:* Draw a picture of your home. Ask children to close their eyes and imagine the front of their home. Is it an apartment building, a cabin, a mobile home, a house, a condominium? How many windows and doors can be seen from the front? Are there flowers, bushes, trees? Draw a picture of your home and include as many details as possible.

My Home

2. *Naive Self-Portrait:* Draw a picture of yourself sitting in a big, comfortable armchair like the one in *A Chair for My Mother.*

Naive Self-Portrait

3. *Street Scene Mural:* Create a class mural of a street scene like the one in *A Chair for My Mother* in which the neighbors bring furniture, toys, cookware, and so on. On separate pieces of 8 x 8–inch paper, students draw, color, and cut out pictures of themselves carrying something to donate. Encourage them to make their bodies the full height of the paper. On mural paper, draw and color a background of storefronts and apartment buildings, along with a wide sidewalk at the bottom of the paper. Glue the student portraits to the sidewalk.

Cartoon Style

Definitions

In a Nutshell

Cartoons are simplistic, and often unrealistic, illustrations created for satire, caricature, or humor.

Taking a Closer Look

From the beginning of time, humans have created simple and sometimes humorous drawings to depict the world around them. On papyrus scrolls, Egyptians painted animals performing human tasks, while Greeks and Romans carved humorous illustrations of grylli—strange beasts made of combinations of animal and human body parts. The margins on illuminated manuscripts from the Middle Ages are filled with drolleries—whimsical beasts and animals. Scrolls created by the Japanese artist Toba Sojo (1052–1140) show animals in human clothing and having human actions.

The history of the word "cartoon" dates back to the Renaissance (1400s–1500s). Renaissance artists planned large works of art, such as frescoes, mosaics, tapestries, and sculptures, by first sketching full-size drawings on heavy paper or board, called *cartone* in Italian. Today, *cartones* by Raphael and da Vinci are displayed in major art collections and are extremely valuable.

In eighteenth-century England, political caricatures began to flourish. The word "caricature" comes from the Italian word *caricatura,* which means "ridiculous portrait." These humorous illustrations were created to make fun of famous and infamous celebrities and politicians. They poked fun at everything from social issues and political scandals to manners and fads.

CHAPTER 17

In 1843 an exhibit of sketches, or cartoons in the historical sense, of proposed decorations for the British Houses of Parliament was opened to the public. *Punch* magazine created its own series of funny sketches poking fun at the exhibit. From then on the word "cartoon" took on the new, and contemporary, meaning of "funny drawings."

The language of cartoons is a universal language. A single cartoon can tell an entire story without words, which allows it to communicate in any language. Cartoons often reflect opinions or ideas about current events and people, and they may attempt to change opinions.

Characteristics of Cartoon Style

1. Very simple drawings
2. Black outline around figures and objects
3. Unrealistic, exaggerated images
4. Follow some, but not all, of the conventions for three-dimensional drawing
5. May be humorous
6. May include personified animals and inanimate objects—animals or objects given human characteristics
7. Simplified, and sometimes stereotypical, understanding of human characteristics

Fine Art Examples

Chic Young (1901–1973): *Blondie*
Gary Larson (1950–): *Far Side*
Charles Schultz (1922–): *Peanuts*

Children's Literature Examples

Henkes, Kevin. *Owen.* New York: Greenwillow Books, 1993.
Rathmann, Peggy. *Officer Buckle and Gloria.* New York: G. P. Putnam's Sons, 1995.
Seuss, Dr. *The Cat in the Hat.* New York: Random House, 1957.

Explorations

Officer Buckle and Gloria

Written and illustrated by Peggy Rathmann

(New York: G. P. Putnam's Sons, 1995)

Officer Buckle was always ignored by the children at Napville Elementary School when he gave his safety speeches until his police dog, Gloria, accompanied him and made the children sit up and listen.

How the Artist Used the Style

In cartoons, animals do things only humans can do. On the inside of the front and back covers and throughout the book, notice the different human things Gloria does—washes paws in the sink, holds up traffic signs, talks on the telephone, wears headphones, and signs autographs. Cartoon characters also do things that are not really possible, such as in the drawing of Gloria pretending to be electrocuted.

Art Exploration: Cartoon

Students draw pictures of animals or inanimate objects doing human things.

Materials

- Drawing paper
- Pencils
- Crayons, colored pencils, or markers

Directions

1. Discuss different human activities students have seen animals or objects (such as teapots, hoses, and candlesticks) do in cartoons, comics, and picture books—wear clothes, drive cars, eat, read books, and so on.
2. Students draw and color pictures of animals or objects doing human activities. Drawings should be simple; they do not need a lot of detail.

Cartoon

Variations

1. *Out-of-Proportion Cartoon:* Make a simple drawing of your body, except choose one body part (head, ears, nose, hand, feet, etc.) and draw it twice as large as the rest of your body.

Out-of-Proportion Cartoon

2. *Cartoon Symmetry:* Find pictures of cartoon characters that are facing forward and are symmetrical—the right side of the face and body mirrors the left side. Cut the character in half from the top to the bottom. Draw the missing side.

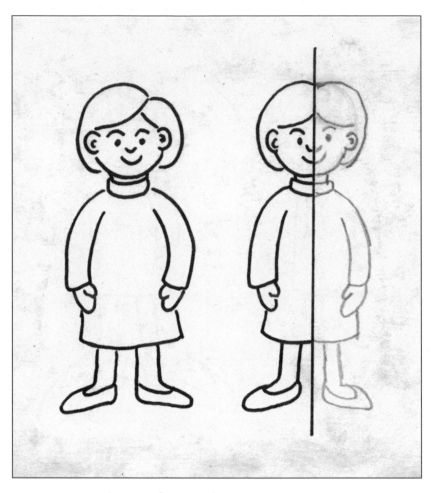

Cartoon Symmetry

3. *Cartoon Nursery Rhyme:* Create a series of three to five small cartoon panels illustrating a nursery rhyme or a poem such as "Little Miss Muffet," "Humpty Dumpty," or "Hey, Diddle-Diddle."

Cartoon Nursery Rhyme

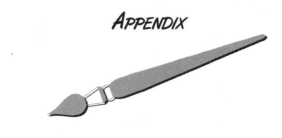

Art Resource Books

Teaching Art Elements and Design Principles

Evans, Joy, and Jo Ellen Moore. *How to Teach Art to Children.* Monterey, Calif.: Evan-Moor Educational Publishers, 1992.

Designed for teachers of first through sixth grades, this book provides large-group, small-group, and independent project experiences in color concepts, pattern and design concepts, line and shape concepts, and texture concepts. Also included are suggestions of children's literature and fine art examples of the concepts introduced.

Klaustermeier, Del. *Art Ideas for the Elementary Classroom.* Denver: Libraries Unlimited, 1997.

More than 120 activities are described in this book. The activities are based on composition, line, area, texture, value, color, space, and three-dimensional construction. In addition to an example of the finished artwork, each activity lists the design element used, the art history reference, and recommended grade level.

Wolfersperger, Shirley Kay, and Eloise Carlston. *Experimenting with Art.* Glenview, Ill.: Good Year Books/Scott Foresman, 1992.

For teachers of third through sixth grades, this book has twenty-five easy-to-teach lessons in the elements of art and the principles of design. Creative reproducible art worksheets are included for each lesson. Also included are lists of famous paintings that correlate to the concepts taught in each lesson.

Teaching Drawing

The following four books were written to teach anyone to draw. Although the specific techniques used by each author are very different, there is a common thread—anyone can learn to draw and draw well!

Brookes, Mona. *Drawing with Children.* Los Angeles: J. P. Tarcher, 1986

Mona Brookes's method teaches children to see and recognize five basic elements of shape. These elements are used to draw the contour edges (outline) of objects and the spaces between them. By knowing and recognizing these five elements, a student has all the information he or she needs to re-create any shape on a piece of paper. After the contour shape is drawn, volume and shading are added.

Brookes has perfected the technique of "guided drawing," which requires providing very specific information to students during the drawing lesson. The teacher draws an object, line by line, explaining the type of line he or she is using, how big or how small, short or long, what direction it is going, and what its relationship to other lines is. As he or she draws a line, providing specific information about it, the students watch. They then attempt to duplicate the line on their paper. The purpose of this technique is to talk students into seeing the way an artist sees. The end result, after guiding students through a number of drawings, is that they begin to "self-talk" themselves through their own drawings.

Edwards, Betty. *Drawing on the Right Side of the Brain.* Los Angeles: J. P. Tarcher, 1979.

Edwards's goal is to help people learn to see the way artists see, with the ultimate goal of drawing the way artists draw. According to the author, "You may feel that you are seeing things just fine and that it's the drawing that is hard. But the opposite is true, and the exercises in this book are designed to help you make the mental shift and gain a twofold advantage: first, to open access by conscious volition to the right side of your brain in order to experience a slightly altered mode of awareness; second, to see things in a different way. Both will enable you to draw well" (p. 4).

McIntyre, Bruce. *Drawing Textbook.* Self-published, 1994, 1014 Wright St., Santa Ana, California.

Kistler, Mark. *Mark Kistler's Draw Squad.* New York: Simon & Schuster, 1988.

Bruce McIntyre was Mark Kistler's teacher and mentor. McIntyre identified seven laws of perspective; Kistler expanded on these concepts to come up with his "Ten Key Words." Their approach to teaching drawing is to explain these key concepts so that students understand what they are seeing. The better we understand what we are seeing, the more able we are to draw three-dimensionally. The concepts of these two authors are:

- *Foreshortening:* "squishing" or flattening objects
- *Contour lines:* giving shape to curved surfaces
- *Overlapping:* drawing an object in front of another object
- *Surface:* drawing objects higher or lower on the paper
- *Shading:* adding darkness opposite the light source
- *Shadows:* the darkness caused by an object
- *Density:* darker, more detailed objects look closer
- *Size:* bigger objects look closer

Teaching Cartooning

Hamm, Jack. *Cartooning the Head & Figure.* New York: Perigee Books/Putnam Publishing Group, 1967.

This is one of the most complete books on cartooning available. With more than 3,000 illustrations, it includes step-by-step procedures for drawing cartoons. It also provides a thorough study of how to express a wide range of emotions with facial expressions and body language, as well as hundreds of variations of cartooning styles.

Bibliography

Batterberry, Ariane Ruskin, and Michael Batterberry. *The Pantheon Story of American Art for Young People.* New York: Pantheon Books, 1976.

Brookes, Mona. *Drawing with Children.* Los Angeles: J. P. Tarcher, 1986.

Canaday, John. *What Is Art?* New York: McGraw–Hill, 1980.

Core Knowledge Sequence, Content Guidelines for Grades K–6. Rev. ed. Charlottesville, Va.: Core Knowledge Foundation, 1995.

Courthion, Pierre. *Impressionism.* Translated by John Shepley. New York: Harry N. Abrams, 1997.

Diamond, David G., ed. *The Bulfinch Pocket Dictionary of Art Terms,* 3d ed. Boston: Bulfinch Press/Little, Brown, 1992.

Edwards, Betty. *Drawing on the Right Side of the Brain.* Los Angeles: J. P. Tarcher, 1979.

Encyclopedia of Art, Volume 8. New York: Greystone Press, 1968.

Evans, Joy, and Jo Ellen Moore. *How to Teach Art to Children.* Monterey, Calif.: Evan–Moor Educational Publishers, 1992.

Gardner, Helen. *Gardner's Art Through the Ages,* 7th ed. Vols. 1 and 2. New York: Harcourt Brace Jovanovich, 1980.

Hamm, Jack. *Cartooning the Head & Figure.* New York: Perigee Books/Putnam Publishing Group, 1967.

Heller, Nancy G. *Women Artists: An Illustrated History.* New York: Abbeville Press, 1987.

Keener, Polly. *Cartooning.* Englewood Cliffs, N.J.: Prentice–Hall, 1992.

Kistler, Mark. *Mark Kistler's Draw Squad.* New York: Simon & Schuster, 1988.

Klaustermeier, Del. *Art Ideas for the Elementary Classroom.* Denver: Libraries Unlimited, 1997.

Lahti, N. E. *Plain Talk About Art.* New York: York Books, 1988.

Lipman, Jean, and Tom Armstrong, eds. *American Folk Painters of Three Centuries.* New York: Hudson Hills Press, 1980.

McIntyre, Bruce. *Drawing Textbook.* Santa Ana, Calif.: self-published, 1994.

Metropolitan Seminars in Art, Portfolio 2, Realism. Philadelphia: Metropolitan Museum of Art, 1958.

Metropolitan Seminars in Art, Portfolio 3, Expressionism. Philadelphia: Metropolitan Museum of Art, 1958.

Murray, Peter and Linday. *Penguin Dictionary of Art and Artists,* 7th ed. London: Penguin Books, 1997.

Ocvirk, Otto, Robert Bone, Robert Stinson, and Philip Wigg. *Art Fundamentals, Theory and Practice,* 5th ed. Dubuque, Ia.: Wm. C. Brown Publishers, 1985.

Simmons, Seymour, III, and Marc S. A. Winer. *Drawing: The Creative Process.* New York: Prentice–Hall Press, 1977.

Sparkes, Roy. *Teaching Art Basics.* London: BT Batsford Limited, 1973.

Weismann, Donald L. *The Visual Arts as Human Experience.* Englewood Cliffs, N.J.: Prentice Hall, 1970.

Wolfersperger, Shirley Kay, and Eloise Carlston. *Experimenting with Art.* Glenview, Ill.: Good Year Books/Scott Foresman, 1992.

The World Book Encyclopedia. "Painting." Chicago, Ill.: Field Enterprises Educational, 1966.

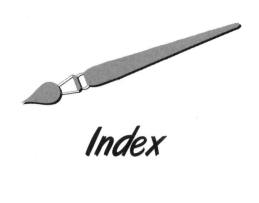

Index

Book Titles, Authors, and Illustrators

Book Titles, Authors, and Illustrators
continued

Book Titles, Authors, and Illustrators
continued

Art Elements, Design Principles, Artistic Styles, and Terms

Art Elements, Design Principles, Artistic Styles, and Terms
continued

Art Explorations

Art Explorations

continued

Art Explorations
continued